Orthodox Anglican Priest's Manual

ISBN: 978-0-578-01297-1

"I love Jesus (UKJV)."

Table of Contents

The Orthodox Anglican Priest's Manual

Forward

The offices for the sick and dying are the forgotten child of the Book of Common Prayer. The rubric has not been updated since 1549, but much has changed since then. People go to hospitals and nursing homes instead of taking to their bed. With longer life spans and modern medicine, people are living longer and often experience more and longer hospitalizations. Other jurisdictions updated their books in the 1960's, but the results were mixed and difficult to use.

Visitation of the Sick has been shortened to reflect use in a hospital or nursing home instead of at home.

The Reserved Sacrament is usually preferable when ministering to the sick.

The Communion Service is intended for use by chaplains and parish clergy during visits to hospitals, nursing homes, and assisted living facilities. It is a modern translation of the 1928 BCP as shortened by the 1549 rubric. Orthodox and Roman Catholic clergy have provided unofficial help in preparing it. Where there were questions, the Sarum Missal was used as a reference, since the whole undivided Church considers it valid. This Liturgy is also acceptable to some Protestant chaplains, as was the 1928 BCP. It could be used outside of chaplaincy by omitting the Prayer for Healing and replacing the Opening Prayer and Lessons with those appointed in the Lectionary. Episcopal approval for this would, of course, have to be obtained, since the 1549 rubric only applies to the sick.

The UKJV, a slightly modernized KJV, has been used for Scripture quotations except for the Psalms. Chaplains have found that many of those who are dying like to have the Psalms read to them, so the Psalter has been included from the 1928 BCP (except for Psalm 23, which is KJV). The use of this translation follows the Anglican practice since 1549.

Rev. Paul Taylor, LL.M.

The Order for the Visitation of the Sick

The following Service, or any part thereof, may be used at the discretion of the Priest.

As the Priest comes into the sick person's presence, he says:
Peace be unto you.

Let us pray.

Lord, have mercy upon us.
Christ, have mercy upon us.
Lord, have mercy upon us.

Our Father, Who art in heaven, Hallowed be Thy Name. Thy kingdom come. Thy will be done, on earth as it is in heaven. Give us this day our daily bread. And forgive us our trespasses, as we forgive those who trespass against us. And lead us not into temptation, but deliver us from evil. Amen.

Dominus regit me   Psalm 23

The Lord is my shepherd; I shall not want. He maketh me to lie down in green pastures: He leadeth me beside the still waters. He restoreth my soul: He leadeth me in the paths of righteousness for His Name's sake. Yea, though I walk through the valley of the shadow of death, I will fear no evil: for Thou art with me; Thy rod and Thy staff they comfort me. Thou preparest a table before me in the presence of mine enemies: Thou anointest my head with oil; my cup runneth over. Surely goodness and mercy shall follow me all the days of my life: and I will dwell in the house of the Lord for ever. Amen.

Prayer for Healing

O God, the strength of the weak and those who suffer: Mercifully accept our prayers, and grant to Your servant, *N*, the help of Your power, that *his* sickness may be turned into health, and our sorrow into joy; through Jesus Christ our Lord. *Amen.*

If the sick person desires to make his confession, the following form may be used. If not, the service continues.
Let us, therefore, confess our sins to the Lord and to each other. *Jas 5:16.*

Silence may be kept.

Priest and People together, all kneeling:
O Almighty Father, Lord of heaven and earth, we confess that we have sinned against You in thought, word, and deed. Have mercy upon us, O God, after Your great goodness; according to the multitude of Your mercies, do away our offenses and cleanse us from our sins; for Jesus Christ's sake. Amen.

OR if the time is short:
I confess all my sins both known and unknown.

Absolution by the Priest

Priest:
The Almighty and merciful Lord grant you **X** Absolution and Remission of all your sins, true repentance, amendment of life, and the grace and consolation of His Holy Spirit. *Amen.*

Unto God's gracious mercy and protection we commit you. The Lord bless you, and keep you. The Lord make His face to shine upon you, and be gracious unto you. The Lord lift up His countenance upon you, and give you peace, both now and evermore (*Num 6:24-26*). *Amen.*

In Time of Great Sickness and Mortality

Almighty God, in this time of grievous sickness, we come to You for strength and relief. Deliver us from our peril; give strength and skill to all those who minister to the sick; through Jesus Christ our Lord. *Amen.*

For a Sick Person

Almighty God, our only help in time of need; We humbly ask You to visit, and relieve Your sick servant, *N*, for whom our prayers are desired. Look upon *him* with the eyes of Your mercy; strengthen *him* with a sense of Your goodness; preserve *him* from the temptations of the enemy; and give *him* patience under *his* affliction. Enable *him* to lead the residue of *his* life in Your fear, and to Your glory; and grant that finally *he* may dwell with You in life everlasting; through Jesus Christ our Lord. *Amen.*

Prayer for the Sick

O Lord Jesus Christ, our God, Who by Your word healed all diseases; Who raised the mother-in-law of Your chosen Disciple, Peter, from her sickbed; Who in Your pity and goodness bears all our infirmities: Come now to help Thy servant, *N.* Heal *him* of every sickness which afflicts *him.* Raise *him* from this malady and send down upon *him* Your great mercy and, if it is Your will, grant *him* health and a complete recovery. For You are the Physician of our souls and bodies, and unto You we ascribe glory, together with Your Father Who is from everlasting, and Your all-holy, and good, and life-creating Spirit. *Amen.*

For a Sick Child

O Heavenly Father, watch over the sick child, *N*, for whom our prayers are offered, and grant that *he* may be restored to that perfect health which it is Yours alone to give; through Jesus Christ our Lord. *Amen.*

For a Person under Affliction

O Merciful God, Who has taught us in Your holy Word that You do not willingly afflict or grieve the children of men: Look with pity, we beseech You, upon the sorrows of Your servant, *N*, for Whom our prayers are offered; through Jesus Christ our Lord. *Amen.*

For the Recovery of a Sick Person

O Merciful God, giver of life and health: Bless, we pray You, Your servant, *N*, and those who administer to *him* of Your healing gifts; that *he* may be restored to health of body and of mind; through Jesus Christ our Lord. *Amen.*

For One About to Undergo an Operation

Almighty God, we ask You to strengthen Your servant in *his* suffering, and to bless the means made use of for *his* cure. Fill *his* heart with confidence, that though *he* be sometime afraid, *he* yet may put *his* trust in You; through Jesus Christ our Lord. *Amen.*

Prayer of St. Luke

Almighty God, Who inspired Your servant St. Luke, the Physician, to set forth in the Gospel the love and healing power of Your Son: Manifest in Your Church the like power and love, to the healing of our bodies and our souls; through the same Your Son Jesus Christ our Lord. *Amen.*

Living In Order to Die Well Anytime

While the content of this prayer is perfectly appropriate for the chronically sick, it may also be said by mourners at a funeral.

O God, Whose days are without end, and Whose mercies cannot be numbered: Make us, we beseech You, deeply sensible of the shortness and uncertainty of human life, and let Your Holy Spirit lead us in holiness and righteousness all our days; that, when we shall have served You in our generation, we may be gathered unto our fathers, having the testimony of a good conscience; in the communion of the Universal Church; in the confidence of a certain faith, in the comfort of a reasonable, religious, and holy hope; in favor with You our God, and in perfect charity with the world. All which we ask through Jesus Christ our Lord. *Amen.*

When Sickness Increases

O Lord Jesus Christ our Savior, You were born for our sake, for our sake You hungered and thirsted, for our sake You suffered and gave Your life over to death. As Your servant, *N*, now shares in Your sufferings, may *he* also share in Your grace. May Your precious Blood wash away the stains of *his* sins. May Your righteousness cleanse away *his* unrighteousness. Look not upon *his* works, but rather upon *his* faith in You when *he* stands before You as Judge. As *his* sickness increases, so increase to *him* Your plenteous grace. Let not *his* faith waver, nor *his* hope fail, nor *his* love wax cold; let not the dread of death cause *him* to cast away *his* trust in You, nor to place it anywhere but in You but, looking steadfastly to You even to the last, let *him* say, "Into Your hands, O Lord, I commend my spirit," and so enter into everlasting joy with You in the Kingdom of the Father, and of the Son, and of the Holy Spirit: one God, world without end. *Amen.*

Before an Operation

O Lord Jesus Christ our God, Who patiently endured the wounding of Your sacred Body, that You might save the souls and bodies of Your people: Look graciously upon the suffering body of this Your servant, *N*, and strengthen *him* to bear patiently whatever You shall see fit to give *him*. Bless the means of *his* cure. Grant that *he* may so endure *his* sufferings in the flesh and be restored to health. *Amen*.

After an Accident or For One Injured in Body

O Lord God our Savior, Who is the Great Physician,the Deliverer from pain: Mercifully grant Your help and healing to this Your servant, *N*, who has suffered grievous injury of body, and grant that *he*, calling upon You in faith, may be restored by Your loving-kindness. *Amen*.

After an Attempted Suicide

Almighty God, the Creator and Redeemer of mankind, Who give us our life in this world that we may prepare for the life to come, Who have delivered Your servant, *N*, from blood-guiltiness: Have pity, we ask You, upon *him*, who would rashly have thrown away Your gift and, as You have in mercy defeated *his* designs, so grant to *him* time and grace for repentance. Graciously look upon *him*, and in Your compassion forgive *him* what *he* has done amiss through the malice of the Enemy. Restore *him* by Your grace, strengthen *him* with Your might, and bring forth from *his* heart tears of sorrow, that *he* may weep for *his* sins committed against You and, by Your mercy, obtain pardon for them: For You are the God of the penitent, and to You we send up glory, to the Father, and to the Son, and to the Holy Spirit. *Amen*.

Thanksgiving for Relief through an Operation

Almighty God, we thank You for Your compassion in having preserved and healed Your servant, *N*, and that the good work begun in *him* may be fulfilled in Your good pleasure, and that *he* may be brought to everlasting life; through the grace of Your Only-begotten Son. *Amen.*

Thanksgiving for Recovery

O Lord Jesus Christ, the Life and Strength of all who put their trust in You, We give You hearty thanks for restoring Your servant to bodily health so endue *his* soul with all heavenly graces, and perseverance in good works, and prepare us by Your blessings in this life for the enjoyment of eternal happiness in the life to come. *Amen.*

Prayer for a Woman in Labor at Childbirth

We ask You now, Who love mankind, to bless this Your handmaiden, *N*, who is with child, granting her help and comfort at this trying time; ease her labor, and bring her to safe delivery. Yea, O Lord, open the treasury of Your mercies, and Your compassion unto
her, and let her give birth to a fruitful vine, to be a cause of joy to her all the days of her life. *Amen.*

Prayer on the First Day after Childbirth

O Master, Lord Almighty, Who heals every sickness and every weakness: So now, heal this Your handmaiden, *N*, who has given birth. Preserve her and this child which she has borne. Cover her with the shelter of Your wings from this day until her last, through the intercessions of the Most-holy Mary and of all the Saints. *Amen.*

Prayer for a Woman after a Miscarriage

Almighty God, according to Your great mercy, have mercy now on this, Your handmaiden, *N*, whose child has died. Cleanse all her sins, and protect her from every oppression of the devil. By Your great mercy lead her to recovery. *Amen.*

Form of Baptism in an Emergency

Immerse, pour, or immerse three times while saying:
N, you are baptized in the Name of the Father, and of the Son, and of the Holy Spirit. *Amen.*

Conditional Baptism

If there is any doubt whether or not Holy Baptism has previously been administered, the following form is used:
The servant of God, *N*, if not already baptized, is baptized in the Name of the Father, and of the Son, and of the Holy Spirit. *Amen.*

Office at the Adoption of Children

The child who desires to be born again as a son or daughter stands within the doors of the Holy Sanctuary, and he who wishes to receive *him* as such stands outside. Both hold lighted candles in their hands.

The Priest in his vestments, begins:
The Lord be with you.
And also with you.
Let us pray.

O Lord our God, Who by Your beloved child, our Lord Jesus Christ, called us children of God through adoption and the grace of Your omnipotent and Holy Spirit, and said, I will be to him a Father, and he shall be to me a Son: Do You, the Same King, Who loves mankind, look down from

Your holy dwelling place upon these Your servants and unite their natures, which You have begotten separated one from another according to the flesh, through Your Holy Spirit, into father and *son*; Confirm them in Your love; bind them through Your benediction; bless them to Your glory; strengthen them in Your faith, preserving them always, and do not renounce them for what proceeds from out of their lips. Be the mediator for their promises: that their love which they have confessed to You be not torn asunder even to the end of their lives, and be kept sincerely, alive in You our only living and true God, and grant them to be heirs of Your kingdom: For unto You are due all glory, honor and worship, to the Father, and to the Son, and to the Holy Spirit, now and ever, and unto ages of ages. *Amen.*

O Master and Lord, Who are the Maker of all creatures, Who by the first Adam made the bonds of kinship according to the natural flesh, and through Christ Jesus, Your beloved Son and our God, by grace showed us also as Your kindred; these Your servants bow their heads unto You, Who alone know all things even before they happen, and ask of You a blessing, and that in You they may receive that for which they hope: the bond, inscribed in each other, of father and *son*; and that, living worthily in You in adoption to *sonship*, they may keep themselves in due constancy; that, as in all things, so in this may be glorified Your Name, of the Father, and of the Son, and of the Holy Spirit, now and ever. *Amen.*

The father receives his *son* from the Sanctuary, and says:
Today you are my *son*, this day I have begotten you.

The father raises *him* up, and they kiss each other.

The Priest pronounces the Blessing and Dismissal.

Communion from the Reserved Sacrament

Confession

If the Penitent is able to make *his* confession, the Priest says:
Let us confess our sins to the Lord and to each other (*Jas 5:16*).

If the Penitent's condition permits, the Priest rehearses the confession with *him:*
O Almighty Father, Lord of heaven and earth, we confess that we have sinned against You in thought, word, and deed. Have mercy upon us, O God, after Your great goodness; according to the multitude of Your mercies, do away our offenses and cleanse us from our sins; for Jesus Christ's sake. Amen.

OR, if time is short, the Priest only rehearses:
I confess all my sins both known and unknown.

OR, if the Penitent is mortally ill and death is imminent, the Priest only says the Prayer of Absolution.

Absolution

Priest:
The Almighty and merciful Lord grant you **X** Absolution and Remission of all your sins, true repentance, amendment of life, and the grace and consolation of His Holy Spirit. *Amen.*

Communion

The priest may deliver communion in either or both species, as appropriate:

For the Body:
The Body of Christ which was given for you, preserve your body and soul unto everlasting life. *Amen.*

For the Blood:
The Blood of Christ which was shed for you, preserve your body and soul unto everlasting life. *Amen.*

For the Body and the Blood together:
The Body and Blood of Christ which were given and shed for you, preserve your body and soul unto everlasting life. *Amen.*

Unction of the Sick and Dying

O blessed Redeemer, we ask you to relieve by Your indwelling power the distress of Your servant. Release *him* from sin and drive away all *his* pain and suffering: that, being restored to soundness of body and mind, *he* may offer to You praise and thanks. Through Jesus Christ our Lord. *Amen.*

I anoint you with oil and I lay my hands on you in the Name of the Father, and of the Son and of the Holy Spirit, asking for you the mercy of our Lord Jesus Christ: that all pain and sickness of body being put to flight, the blessing of health be with you. *Amen.*

Communion Service

All stand as the the Priest says the following or another appropriate Sentence of Scripture:
The Lord is in His holy temple: Let all the earth keep silence before Him (*Hab 2:20*).

Processional Hymn

The People stand and may sing a hymn as the Priest and other ministers (if any) walk to the Altar.

Prayer for Purity

The People kneel as the Priest prays with raised hands:
Almighty God, unto Whom all hearts are open, all desires known, and from Whom no secrets are hidden: Cleanse the thoughts of our hearts by the inspiration of Your Holy Spirit, that we may perfectly love You and worthily magnify Your holy Name. Through Christ our Lord. *Amen.*

Summary of the Law

Hear what our Lord Jesus Christ says:

"You shall love the Lord your God with all your heart, and with all your soul, and with all your mind. This is the first and great Commandment. And the second is like it: you shall love your neighbor as yourself. On these two Commandments hang all the Law and the Prophets." *Mt 22:37-40.*

"Think not that I am come to destroy the Law, or the Prophets: I am not come to destroy, but to fulfill. For verily I say unto you, 'Till heaven and earth pass, one jot or one tittle shall in no wise pass from the law, till all be fulfilled.'" *Mt 5:17-18.* "Not every one that says unto me, 'Lord, Lord,' shall enter into the Kingdom of Heaven, but he that does the will of My Father Which is in heaven." *Mt 7:21.*

Kyrie

Lord, have mercy.		Kyrie eleison.
Christ, have mercy.	or	*Christe eleison.*
Lord, have mercy.		Kyrie eleison.

Opening Prayer

The Lord be with you.
And also with you.
Let us pray.

Almighty, everliving God, Maker of mankind, Who corrects those whom You love, and chastises everyone whom You receive: We beseech You to have mercy upon this Your *servant* visited with Your hand, and to grant that *he* may take *his* sickness patiently and recover *his* bodily health, if it be Your gracious will; and that, whenever *his* soul shall depart from the body, it may be without spot presented to You; through Jesus Christ our Lord. *Amen.*

OR, if more appropriate:
O Lord, holy Father, by Whose loving-kindness our souls and bodies are renewed: Mercifully look upon Your *servant*; that every cause of sickness being removed, *he* may be restored to soundness of health; through Jesus Christ our Lord. *Amen.*

A Prayer for Healing

Visit this house, O Lord: bless and comfort all within it, restoring to health those infirm of mind or body and granting eternal rest to the departed. Accept them and their suffering into Your loving hands: that, united with Your own suffering and death for the redemption of the world, they shall be united with You, Who conquered death in Your glorious Resurrection and lives and reigns with Your Father in the Unity of the Holy Spirit, one God, world without end. *Amen.*

Epistle

The People sit as the Epistle Lesson is announced:
A reading from the Epistle to the Hebrews.

Despise not the chastening of the Lord, nor faint when you are rebuked by Him: For whom the Lord loves He chastens, and scourges every son whom He receives. *Heb 12:5-6.*

OR, if more appropriate:
A reading from the First Epistle of St. John.

These things have I written to you that believe on the Name of the Son of God; that all of you may know that all of you have eternal life, and that all of you may believe on the Name of the Son of God. And this is the confidence that we have in Him, that, if we ask any thing according to His will, He hears us: And if we know that He hear us, whatsoever we ask, we know that we have the petitions that we desired of Him. *I Jn 5:13-15.*

After the Epistle Lesson:
This is the Word of the Lord.
Thanks be to God.

A hymn may be sung.

Gospel

All stand as the Gospel Lesson is announced:
A reading from the Holy Gospel of our Lord Jesus Christ According to St. John.
Glory to you, Lord Christ.

Verily, verily, I say to you, he that hears my word, and believes on Him that sent Me, has everlasting life, and shall not come into condemnation; but is passed from death to life. *Jn 5:24.*

OR, if more appropriate:
Verily, verily, I say to you, he that believes on Me has everlasting life. I am that bread of life. Your fathers ate manna in the wilderness, and are dead. This is the bread which comes down from heaven, that a man may eat thereof, and not die. I am the living bread which came down from heaven: if any man eat of this bread, he shall live for ever: and the bread that I will give is My flesh, which I will give for the life of the world. *Jn 6:47-51.*

This is the Gospel of the Lord.
Praise to You, Lord Christ.

Nicene Creed

Priest and People together:
I believe in one God, the Father Almighty, Maker of heaven and earth, and of all things visible and invisible; And in one Lord Jesus Christ, the only-begotten Son of God; begotten of His Father before all worlds; God of God; Light of Light; Very God of Very God; begotten, not made; being of one substance with the Father; by Whom all things were made. Who, for us and for our salvation, came down from heaven, and was incarnate by the Holy Spirit of the Virgin Mary, and was made man; And was crucified also for us under Pontius Pilate. He suffered and was buried; and the third day He rose again, according to the Scriptures; And ascended into heaven, and sits at the right hand of the Father; And He will come again with glory to judge both the living and the dead; Whose kingdom shall have no end.

And I believe in the Holy Spirit, the Lord, and Giver of Life, who proceeds from the Father; Who, with the Father and the Son together, is worshiped and glorified; Who spoke by the Prophets. And I believe One Holy Catholic and Apostolic Church. I acknowledge one Baptism for the remission of sins. And I look for the Resurrection of the dead and the Life of the world to come. Amen.

Sermon and Announcements

The People sit for the announcements (if any). A hymn may be sung, followed by the Sermon.

Offertory

A hymn may be sung while the Priest prepares the Altar and offerings. He lifts the burse off the top of the chalice, extracts the corporal from it, sets the burse on the far Gospel side, and then sets the corporal on top of the burse. After lifting off the chalice veil, he folds it on the far Epistle side, removes the ciborium veil and sets it on the chalice veil, unfolds the corporal in the middle of the Altar and spreads it even with the front edge.

The Priest brings the chalice, purificator, and paten to the credenza, if there be one, where he pours wine into the chalice and then makes the sign of the Cross over the uncovered water cruet, blessing it:

The Lord, from **X** Whose side came forth blood and water: by Him be it blessed.

After pouring water in the form of the Cross into the chalice, the Priest removes any drops of water separated from the wine with the purificator, places the required number of breads in the ciborium (or under the Priest's Host on the paten) and sets the paten (covered with the pall) back upon the chalice. Taking up the chalice with the folded purificator at the node, the Priest places it in the center of the corporal, sets the ciborium (if used) behind and to the Epistle side of it, and then places the purificator, pall, and ciborium cover outside the corporal on the Epistle side.

When an offering is presented, the Priest accepts it and may say:

All things come from You, O Lord, and of Your own we have given You (*I Chron 29:14*).

Alternatively, the Priest and People may say or sing:

Doxology

Praise God, from Whom all blessings flow;
Praise Him, all creatures here below;

Praise Him above, ye heavenly host;
Praise Father, Son, and Holy Ghost.

Prayers of the People

Let us pray for the whole state of Christ's Church.

Almighty and everliving God, Who by Your holy Apostle taught us to make prayers and supplications, and to give thanks for all men: We humbly beseech You most mercifully to accept our oblations and to receive these our prayers, which we offer to Your Divine Majesty, beseeching You to inspire continually the Universal Church with the spirit of truth, unity and concord, and grant that all those who do confess Your holy Name may agree in the truth of Your holy Word and live in unity and godly love. We beseech You also so to direct and dispose the hearts of all Christian Rulers: that they may truly and impartially administer justice, to the punishment of wickedness and vice, and to the maintenance of Your true religion and virtue. Give grace, O heavenly Father, to all Bishops and other Ministers: that they may, both by their life and doctrine, set forth Your true and lively Word, and rightly and duly administer Your holy Sacraments. And to all Your People give Your heavenly grace, and especially to this congregation here present: that, with meek heart and due reverence, they may hear and receive Your holy Word, truly serving You in holiness and righteousness all the days of their life. And we most humbly beseech You, of Your goodness, O Lord, to strengthen and give relief to all those who, in this transitory life, are in trouble, sorrow, need, sickness, or any other adversity. And we also bless Your holy Name for all Your servants departed this life in Your

24

faith and fear, beseeching You to grant them continual growth in Your love and service, and to give us grace so to follow their good examples: that with them we may be partakers of Your heavenly kingdom. Grant this, O Father, for Jesus Christ's sake, our only Mediator and Advocate. *Amen.*

The Priest lowers the chalice back onto the center of the corporal, removes the paten and places it in front of the chalice, places the cover on the ciborium, and covers the chalice with the pall.

Exhortation

You who truly and earnestly repent of your sins and are in love and charity with your neighbors and intend to lead a new life, following the commandments of God and walking from henceforth in His holy ways: Draw near with faith, take this holy Sacrament to strengthen you, and make your humble confession to Almighty God, devoutly kneeling.

General Confession

Priest and People, all kneeling:
O Almighty Father, Lord of heaven and earth, we confess that we have sinned against You in thought, word, and deed. Have mercy upon us, O God, after Your great goodness; according to the multitude of Your mercies, do away our offenses and cleanse us from our sins; for Jesus Christ's sake. Amen.

Absolution of Sins

Standing, the Priest prays for the People, still kneeling:
The Almighty and merciful Lord grant you **X** Absolution and Remission of all your sins, true repentance, amendment of life, and the grace and consolation of His Holy Spirit. *Amen.*

Hear the assuring words of our Savior Christ to all who truly turn to Him:

"Come unto Me, all you that labor and are heavy laden, and I will give you rest." *Mt 11:28.*

"God so loved the world, that He gave His Only-Begotten Son: that whosoever believes in Him should not perish, but have everlasting life." *Jn 3:16.*

Hear also what St. Paul says: "This is a faithful saying, and worthy of all acceptation: that Christ Jesus came into the world to save sinners." *I Tim 1:15.*

Hear also what St. John says: "If any man sin, we have an advocate with the Father, Jesus Christ the righteous: And He is the full and perfect Atoning Sacrifice for our sins: and not for our's only, but also for the sins of the whole world." *I Jn 2:1-2.*

Sursum Corda

The Lord be with you.
And also with you.
Lift up your hearts.
We lift them up to the Lord.
Let us give thanks to the Lord our God.
It is fitting, just, and right to give Him thanks and praise.

Preface

It is very fitting, right, just, and our duty to always and everywhere give thanks to You, Father Almighty, Creator of heaven and earth.

Proper Preface

The Priest says the Proper Preface, if appointed, and then continues:
And therefore, with Angels and Archangels, and with all the company of Heaven, we magnify Your glorious Name, evermore saying:

Sanctus and Benedictus

Priest and People together:
Holy, holy, holy, Lord God of hosts. Heaven and earth are full of Your glory: Glory be to You, O Lord Most High. Blessed is He Who comes in the Name of the Lord. Hosannah in the highest.

Prayer of Consecration

The Priest uncovers the ciborium, places its cover outside the corporal, and bowing profoundly with joined hands, prays:
All glory be to You, Almighty God, our heavenly Father, that You, of Your tender mercy, gave Your only Son Jesus Christ to suffer death upon the Cross for our redemption, Who there (by His own oblation of Himself once offered) made a full, perfect, and sufficient sacrifice, oblation, and satisfaction for the sins of the whole world, and instituted, and in His holy Gospel commanded us to continue, a perpetual memory of His precious death and sacrifice until His coming again: We beseech You to in all respects bless, approve, ratify, and make this oblation reasonable and acceptable, sending down upon it Your Holy Spirit, the witness of the Passion of Your most dearly beloved Son, our Lord Jesus Christ, that it may become to us His X Body and His X Blood;

For in the night in which He was betrayed, He took bread,

Holding or placing a hand on the Host, the Priest continues:
and when He had given thanks, He broke it, and gave it to His disciples, saying, "Take, eat, this is My Body, which is given for you: Do this in remembrance of Me."

The Priest places the Host on the paten, covers the ciborium, uncovers the Chalice, placing the pall outside the corporal on the Epistle side, and continues:
Likewise, after supper, He took the cup,

Holding or placing a hand on the Chalice, the Priest continues:
and when He had given thanks, He gave it to them, saying, "Drink ye all of this, for this is My Blood of the New Testament, which is shed for you, and for many, for the remission of sins: Do this as oft as ye shall drink it, in remembrance of Me."

The Priest places the Chalice on the corporal, covers it with the pall, stands with hands extended, and continues:
Therefore, O Lord and heavenly Father: According to the institution of Your dearly beloved Son our Savior Jesus Christ, we, Your humble servants, offer to Your Divine Majesty from Your own bounty these **X** gifts on behalf of all.

Bowing with hands joined, the Priest continues:
And we most humbly beseech You, O merciful Father, to hear us and, of Your Almighty goodness, to **X** bless and **X** sanctify with Your Word and Holy Spirit these Your gifts and creatures of bread and wine: that all who receive them may partake of the most sacred Body and Blood of Your Son, be filled with Your grace and heavenly **X** benediction, and in unity as one body with Him, that He may dwell in us, and we in Him, Who lives and reigns with You in the unity of the Holy Spirit, by Whom and with Whom be to You all honor and glory, O Father Almighty, world without end. *Amen.*

Lord's Prayer

And now, as our Savior Jesus Christ taught us, we are bold to pray:

Priest and People together:
Our Father Who is in heaven, holy is Your Name. Your Kingdom come, Your will be done, on earth as it is in heaven. Give us this day our daily bread. And forgive our sins, as we forgive those who sin against us. And lead us not into temptation, but deliver us from evil. For Yours is the Kingdom, and the power, and the glory, for ever and ever. Amen.

Fracture

The Priest uncovers the Chalice, makes the sign of the Cross with the Host over the Chalice, breaks it down the middle and, after pausing a moment, places the right side on the paten, breaks a particle from the bottom of the left side with his right hand and, still holding the particle over the Chalice, places the left side on the paten joined to the right side. Making the sign of the Cross over the Chalice with the particle, the Priest places it in the Chalice as he prays silently.

Prayer of Humble Access

Bowing with hands joined and eyes on the Host, the Priest prays:
We do not presume to come to this Your Table trusting in our own righteousness, merciful Lord, but in Your manifold and great mercies. We are not worthy so much as to gather up the crumbs under Your Table. But You are the same Lord Whose nature is always to have mercy. Grant us therefore, gracious Lord, to eat the Flesh of Your dear Son Jesus Christ and to drink His Blood: that our sinful bodies may be made clean by His Body, our souls washed by His most precious Blood, and we may evermore live in Him and He in us. *Amen.*

Holy Communion

A hymn may be sung as the Priest makes his own communion. He then uncovers the ciborium, takes it up in his left hand at the node and, holding one Host above it, goes to the rail. Making the sign of the Cross with each Host over the ciborium, the Priest communicates the People, saying:
The Body of our Lord Jesus Christ, which was given for you, keep your body and soul in everlasting life.

The Blood of our Lord Jesus Christ, which was shed for you, keep your body and soul in everlasting life.

For the Body and Blood administered together:
The Body and Blood of our Lord Jesus Christ, which was given and shed for you, keep your body and soul in everlasting life.

If necessary, the Priest consecrates additional Bread or Wine using the Prayer of Consecration, beginning at *All glory be to You* ... and ending with ... *His Body and His Blood.*

Prayer of Thanksgiving

Let us pray.

The Priest standing, the People devoutly kneeling:
Almighty and everliving God, we thank You for feeding us with the spiritual food of the most precious Body and Blood of Your Son our Savior Jesus Christ; and for assuring us in these holy Mysteries of Your favor and goodness towards us and that we are living members of the Body of your Son, the blessed company of all faithful people, and are also heirs through hope of Your eternal Kingdom by the merits of His most precious death and passion. Assist us with Your grace, Heavenly Father: that we may continue in that holy fellowship and do the good works that You have prepared for us. Through Jesus Christ our Lord, to Whom, with You and the Holy Spirit, are all honor and glory, world without end. *Amen.*

Gloria in Excelsis

Priest and People together, all standing:
Glory to God in the highest and peace to His people on earth. Lord God, heavenly King, Almighty God and Father: we worship You, we give You thanks, we praise You for Your glory. Lord Jesus Christ, only Son of the Father, Lord God, Lamb of God, Who takes away the sin of the world: Have mercy on us. You Who are seated at the right hand of the Father: Receive our prayer. For You alone are holy, You alone are the Lord, You alone are the Most High: Jesus Christ, with the Holy Spirit, in the glory of God the Father. Amen.

Blessing

The Priest blesses the People, kneeling:
The Peace of God, which passes all understanding, keep your hearts and minds in the knowledge and love of God and of His Son Jesus Christ our Lord, and the Blessing of God Almighty, the Father, the Son, and the Holy Spirit, be with you and remain with you always. *Amen.*

Dismissal

Depart in peace to love and serve the Lord.
Thanks be to God.

Service at a Funeral Home

I am the resurrection and the life, saith the Lord: he that believeth in Me, though he were dead, yet shall he live: and whosoever liveth and believeth in Me, shall never die.

I know that my redeemer liveth, and that He shall stand at the latter day upon the earth: and though this body be destroyed, yet shall I see God: Whom I shall see for myself, and mine eyes shall behold, and not as a stranger.

We brought nothing into this world, and it is certain we can carry nothing out. The Lord gave, and the Lord hath taken away; blessed be the Name of the Lord.

Dominus regit me   Psalm 23

Priest and People together:
The Lord is my shepherd; I shall not want. He maketh me to lie down in green pastures: He leadeth me beside the still waters. He restoreth my soul: He leadeth me in the paths of righteousness for His Name's sake. Yea, though I walk through the valley of the shadow of death, I will fear no evil: for Thou art with me; Thy rod and Thy staff they comfort me. Thou preparest a table before me in the presence of mine enemies: Thou anointest my head with oil; my cup runneth over. Surely goodness and mercy shall follow me all the days of my life: and I will dwell in the house of the Lord for ever.

The Lord be with you.
And also with you.
Let us pray.

Lord, have mercy upon us.
Christ, have mercy upon us.
Lord, have mercy upon us.

Our Father, Who art in heaven, Hallowed be Thy Name. Thy kingdom come. Thy will be done on earth, as it is in heaven. Give us this day our daily bread. And forgive us our trespasses, as we forgive those who trespass against us. And lead us not into temptation; But deliver us from evil. Amen.

The following or other appropriate Prayers are said:
O God, Whose mercies cannot be numbered: Accept our prayers on behalf of the soul of Your servant departed, and grant *him* an entrance into the land of light and joy, in the fellowship of Your saints. Through Jesus Christ our Lord. *Amen.*

Most merciful Father, Who has been pleased to take to Yourself the soul of this Your *servant:* Grant to us who are still in our pilgrimage, and who walk as yet by faith that, having served You with constancy on earth, we may be joined hereafter with Your blessed saints in glory everlasting. Through Jesus Christ our Lord. *Amen.*

O Lord Jesus Christ, Who by Your death took away the sting of death: Grant to us Your servants so to follow in faith where You have led the way, that we may at length fall asleep peacefully in You, and awaken after Your likeness. Through Your mercy, Who lives with the Father and the Holy Spirit, one God, world without end. *Amen.*

Blessing

The Lord bless and keep you: The Lord make His face to shine upon you, and be gracious to you: The Lord lift up His countenance upon You and give you peace, now and for evermore. *Amen.*

This Office is only appropriate for the faithful departed in Christ, provided that in any other case the Minister may, at his discretion, use such part of this Office, or such devotions taken from other parts of this Book, as may be fitting.

Graveside Service

When they come to the grave, while the casket is made ready to be laid into the earth, is sung or said:
Man, that is born of a woman, has but a short time to live, and is full of misery. He comes up, and is cut down, like a flower; he flees as it were a shadow, and never continues in one place.

In the midst of life we are in death; of whom may we seek for aid and assistance, but of You, O Lord, who for our sins art justly displeased?

Yet, O Lord God most holy, O Lord most mighty, O holy and most merciful Savior, deliver us not into the bitter pains of eternal death.

You, Lord, know the secrets of our hearts; shut not Your merciful ears to our prayer; but spare us, Lord most holy, O God most mighty, O holy and merciful Savior, You most worthy Judge eternal, suffer us not, at our last hour, for any pains of death, to fall from You.

Committal

Earth may be cast upon the casket by some standing by, the Priest saying:
Unto Almighty God we commend the soul of our *brother* departed, and we commit *his* body to the ground; earth to earth, ashes to ashes, dust to dust; in sure and certain hope of the Resurrection to eternal life, through our Lord Jesus Christ, at Whose coming in glorious majesty to judge the world, the earth and the sea shall give up their dead; and the corruptible bodies of those who sleep in Him shall

be changed, and made like His own glorious body; according to the mighty working whereby He is able to subdue all things to Himself.

The Priest may say:
May the Angels lead you into Paradise; and the Martyrs receive you at your coming and bring you into the holy city Jerusalem. May the choirs of Angels receive you, and may you, with Lazarus once poor, have everlasting rest. *Amen.*

Remember the word of our Lord Jesus Christ: Blessed are they that mourn for they shall be strengthened. *Amen.*

Our Father, Who art in heaven, Hallowed be Thy Name. Thy kingdom come. Thy will be done on earth, as it is in heaven. Give us this day our daily bread. And forgive us our trespasses, as we forgive those who trespass against us. And lead us not into temptation; But deliver us from evil. Amen.

Blessing

The Lord bless and keep you: The Lord make His face to shine upon you, and be gracious to you: The Lord lift up His countenance upon You and give you peace, now and for evermore. *Amen.*

This Office is only appropriate for the faithful departed in Christ, provided that in any other case the Minister may, at his discretion, use such part of this Office, or such devotions taken from other parts of this Book, as may be fitting.

At the Burial of the Dead at Sea

The same office is used, but with the following Committal:
Unto Almighty God we commend the soul of our *brother* departed, and we commit his body to the deep; in sure and certain hope of the Resurrection to eternal life, through our

Lord Jesus Christ; at Whose coming in glorious majesty to judge the world, the sea shall give up her dead; and the corruptible bodies of those who sleep in Him shall be changed, and made like His glorious body; according to the mighty working whereby He is able to subdue all things unto Himself.

At the Burial of a Child

The Minister meets the casket and goes in front of it either into the church or to the grave, saying:

I am the resurrection and the life, saith the Lord: he that believeth in Me, though he were dead, yet shall he live: and whosoever liveth and believeth in Me, shall never die.

Jesus called them unto him and said, Suffer the little children to come unto me, and forbid them not: for of such is the Kingdom of God.

He shall feed His flock like a shepherd: He shall gather the lambs with His arms, and carry them in His bosom.

When they go into the church, all stand and recite:

Dominus regit me   Psalm 23

The Lord is my shepherd; I shall not want. He maketh me to lie down in green pastures: He leadeth me beside the still waters. He restoreth my soul: He leadeth me in the paths of righteousness for His Name's sake. Yea, though I walk through the valley of the shadow of death, I will fear no evil: for Thou art with me; Thy rod and Thy staff they comfort me. Thou preparest a table before me in the presence of mine enemies: Thou anointest my head with oil; my cup runneth over. Surely goodness and mercy shall follow me all the days of my life: and I will dwell in the house of the Lord for ever.

Gloria Patri

Glory be to the Father, and to the Son, and to the Holy Spirit: *As it was in the beginning, is now, and ever shall be, world without end. Amen.*

Gospel

A reading from the Holy Gospel According to St. Matthew.

At the same time came the Disciples unto Jesus, saying, "Who is the greatest in the Kingdom of Heaven?" And Jesus called a little child unto Him, and set him in the midst of them, and said, "Verily I say unto you, except ye be converted, and become as little children, ye shall not enter into the Kingdom of Heaven. Whosoever therefore shall humble himself as this little child, the same is greatest in the Kingdom of Heaven. And whoso shall receive one such little child in My Name receives Me.... Take heed that ye despise not one of these little ones; for I say unto you, that in heaven their angels do always behold the face of My Father Which is in heaven." *Mt 18:1-5, 10.*

The Lord be with you.
And also with you.
Let us pray.

Lord, have mercy upon us.
Christ, have mercy upon us.
Lord, have mercy upon us.

Minister and People together:
Our Father, Who art in heaven, Hallowed be Thy Name. Thy kingdom come. Thy will be done on earth, as it is in heaven. Give us this day our daily bread. And forgive us our trespasses, as we forgive those who trespass against us. And lead us not into temptation; But deliver us from evil. Amen.

Blessed are the pure in heart;
For they shall see God.

Blessed be the Name of the Lord;
Henceforth, world without end.

Lord, hear our prayer;
And let our cry come unto Thee.

The following or other appropriate Prayers are said:
O merciful Father, Whose face the angels of Your little ones always behold in heaven: Grant that we may steadfastly believe that this Your child has been taken into the safekeeping of Your eternal love. Through Jesus Christ our Lord. *Amen.*

Almighty and merciful Father, Who grants to children an abundant entrance into Your Kingdom: Grant us grace so to conform our lives to their innocency and perfect faith; that, at length, united with them, we may stand in Your presence in fullness of joy. Through Jesus Christ our Lord. *Amen.*

The grace of our Lord Jesus Christ, and the love of God, and the fellowship of the Holy Spirit, be with us all evermore. *Amen.*

When they come to the grave, the Priest says:
Jesus said to His Disciples, "You now therefore have sorrow: but I will see you again, and your heart shall rejoice, and your joy no man can take from you."

While the earth is being shoveled on the casket, the Priest says:
In sure and certain hope of Resurrection to eternal life through our Lord Jesus Christ, we commit the body of this child to the ground. The Lord bless *him* and keep *him*, the Lord make His face to shine upon *him* and be gracious unto *him*, the Lord lift up His countenance upon *him*, and give *him* peace, both now and evermore. *Amen.*

The People say or sing:

Therefore they are before the Throne of God, and serve Him day and night in His temple: and He Who sits on the Throne shall dwell among them.

They shall hunger no more, neither thirst any more; neither shall the sun light on them, nor any heat.

For the Lamb Which is in the midst of the Throne shall feed them, and shall lead them to living fountains of water: and God shall wipe away all tears from their eyes.

The Lord be with you.
And also with you.

Let us pray.

O God, Whose most dear Son took little children into His arms and blessed them: Give us grace, we beseech You, to entrust the soul of this child to Your neverfailing care and love, and bring us all to Your heavenly Kingdom. Through the same Your Son, Jesus Christ our Lord. *Amen.*

Almighty God, Father of mercies and Giver of all comfort: Deal graciously with all those who mourn, we pray You; that, casting every care on You, they may know the consolation of Your love; through Jesus Christ our Lord. *Amen.*

Blessing

May Almighty God, the Father, and the Son, and the Holy Spirit, bless you and keep you, now and for evermore. *Amen.*

The Psalter or Psalms of David

BOOK I

First Day

Morning Prayer

Beatus vir qui non abiit   Psalm 1

1 Blessed is the man that hath not walked in the counsel of the ungodly, nor stood in the way of sinners, * and hath not sat in the seat of the scornful.
2 But his delight is in the law of the Lord; * and in His law will he exercise himself day and night.
3 And he shall be like a tree planted by the water-side, * that will bring forth his fruit in due season.
4 His leaf also shall not wither; * and look, whatsoever he doeth, it shall prosper.
5 As for the ungodly, it is not so with them; * but they are like the chaff, which the wind scattereth away from the face of the earth.
6 Therefore the ungodly shall not be able to stand in the judgment, * neither the sinners in the congregation of the righteous.
7 But the Lord knoweth the way of the righteous; * and the way of the ungodly shall perish.

Quare fremuerunt gentes?   Psalm 2

1 Why do the heathen so furiously rage together? * and why do the people imagine a vain thing?
2 The kings of the earth stand up, and the rulers take counsel together * against the Lord, and against His Anointed:
3 "Let us break Their bonds asunder, * and cast away Their cords from us."

4 He that dwelleth in heaven shall laugh them to scorn: * the Lord shall have them in derision.
5 Then shall He speak unto them in His wrath, * and vex them in His sore displeasure:
6 "Yet have I set My King * upon My holy hill of Zion."
7 "I will rehearse the decree; * the Lord hath said unto Me, 'Thou art My Son, this day have I begotten Thee.
8 Desire of Me, and I shall give Thee the nations for Thine inheritance, * and the utmost parts of the earth for Thy possession.
9 Thou shalt bruise them with a rod of iron, * and break them in pieces like a potter's vessel.'"
10 Be wise now therefore, O ye kings; * be instructed, ye that are judges of the earth.
11 Serve the Lord in fear, * and rejoice unto Him with reverence.
12 Kiss the Son, lest He be angry, and so ye perish from the right way, if His wrath be kindled, yea but a little. * Blessed are all they that put their trust in Him.

Domine, quid multiplicati?   Psalm 3

1 Lord, how are they increased that trouble me! * many are they that rise against me.
2 Many one there be that say of my soul, * "There is no help for him in his God."
3 But Thou, O Lord, art my defender; * Thou art my worship, and the lifter up of my head.
4 I did call upon the Lord with my voice, * and He heard me out of His holy hill.
5 I laid me down and slept, and rose up again; * for the Lord sustained me.
6 I will not be afraid for ten thousands of the people, * that have set themselves against me round about.
7 Up, Lord, and help me, O my God, * for Thou smitest all mine enemies upon the cheek-bone; Thou hast broken the teeth of the ungodly.

8 Salvation belongeth unto the Lord; * and Thy blessing is upon Thy people.

Cum invocarem   Psalm 4

1 Hear me when I call, O God of my righteousness: * Thou hast set me at liberty when I was in trouble; have mercy upon me, and hearken unto my prayer.
2 O ye sons of men, how long will ye blaspheme mine honor, * and have such pleasure in vanity, and seek after falsehood?
3 Know this also, that the Lord hath chosen to Himself the man that is godly; * when I call upon the Lord He will hear me.
4 Stand in awe, and sin not; * commune with your own heart, and in your chamber, and be still.
5 Offer the sacrifice of righteousness, * and put your trust in the Lord.
6 There be many that say, * "Who will show us any good?"
7 Lord, lift Thou up* the light of Thy countenance upon us.
8 Thou hast put gladness in my heart; * yea, more than when their corn and wine and oil increase.
9 I will lay me down in peace, and take my rest; * for it is Thou, Lord, only, that makest me dwell in safety.

Verba mea auribus   Psalm 5

1 Ponder my words, O Lord, * consider my meditation.
2 O hearken Thou unto the voice of my calling, my King and my God: * for unto Thee will I make my prayer.
3 My voice shalt Thou hear betimes, O Lord; * early in the morning will I direct my prayer unto Thee, and will look up.
4 For Thou art the God that hast no pleasure in wickedness; * neither shall any evil dwell with Thee.
5 Such as be foolish shall not stand in Thy sight; * for Thou hatest all them that work iniquity.
6 Thou shalt destroy them that speak lies: * the Lord will

abhor both the blood-thirsty and deceitful man.

7 But as for me, in the multitude of Thy mercy I will come into Thine house; * and in Thy fear will I worship toward Thy holy temple.

8 Lead me, O Lord, in Thy righteousness, because of mine enemies; * make Thy way plain before my face.

9 For there is no faithfulness in their mouth; * their inward parts are very wickedness.

10 Their throat is an open sepulcher; * they flatter with their tongue.

11 Destroy Thou them, O God; let them perish through their own imaginations; * cast them out in the multitude of their ungodliness; for they have rebelled against Thee.

12 And let all them that put their trust in Thee rejoice: * they shall ever be giving of thanks, because Thou defendest them; they that love Thy Name shall be joyful in Thee;

13 For Thou, Lord, wilt give Thy blessing unto the righteous, * and with Thy favorable kindness wilt Thou defend him as with a shield.

Evening Prayer

Domine, ne in furore   Psalm 6

1 O Lord, rebuke me not in Thine indignation, * neither chasten me in Thy displeasure.

2 Have mercy upon me, O Lord, for I am weak; * O Lord, heal me, for my bones are vexed.

3 My soul also is sore troubled: * but, Lord, how long wilt Thou punish me?

4 Turn Thee, O Lord, and deliver my soul; * O save me, for Thy mercy's sake.

5 For in death no man remembereth Thee; * and who will give Thee thanks in the pit?

6 I am weary of my groaning; * every night wash I my bed, and water my couch with my tears.

7 My beauty is gone for very trouble, * and worn away

because of all mine enemies.

8 Away from me, all ye that work iniquity; * for the Lord hath heard the voice of my weeping.

9 The Lord hath heard my petition; * the Lord will receive my prayer.

10 All mine enemies shall be confounded, and sore vexed; * they shall be turned back, and put to shame suddenly.

Domine, Deus meus Psalm 7

1 O Lord my God, in Thee have I put my trust: * save me from all them that persecute me, and deliver me;

2 Lest he devour my soul like a lion, and tear it in pieces, * while there is none to help.

3 O Lord my God, if I have done any such thing; * or if there be any wickedness in my hands;

4 If I have rewarded evil unto him that dealt friendly with me; * (yea, I have delivered him that without any cause is mine enemy;)

5 Then let mine enemy persecute my soul, and take me; * yea, let him tread my life down upon the earth, and lay mine honor in the dust.

6 Stand up, O Lord, in Thy wrath, and lift up Thyself, because of the indignation of mine enemies; * arise up for me in the judgment that Thou hast commanded.

7 And so shall the congregation of the peoples come about Thee: * for their sakes therefore lift up Thyself again.

8 The Lord shall judge the peoples: give sentence with me, O Lord, * according to my righteousness, and according to the innocence that is in me.

9 O let the wickedness of the ungodly come to an end; * but guide Thou the just.

10 For the righteous God * trieth the very hearts and reins.

11 My help cometh of God, * Who preserveth them that are true of heart.

12 God is a righteous Judge, strong, and patient; * and God is provoked every day.

13 If a man will not turn, He will whet His sword; * He hath bent His bow, and made it ready.
14 He hath prepared for Him the instruments of death; * He ordaineth His arrows against the persecutors.
15 Behold, the ungodly travaileth with iniquity; * he hath conceived mischief, and brought forth falsehood.
16 He hath graven and digged up a pit, * and is fallen himself into the destruction that he made for other.
17 For his travail shall come upon his own head, * and his wickedness shall fall on his own pate.
18 I will give thanks unto the Lord, according to His righteousness; * and I will praise the Name of the Lord Most High.

Domine, Dominus noster　　　　　Psalm 8

1 O Lord our Governor, how excellent is Thy Name in all the world; * Thou that hast set Thy glory above the heavens!
2 Out of the mouth of very babes and sucklings hast Thou ordained strength, because of Thine enemies, * that Thou mightest still the enemy and the avenger.
3 When I consider Thy heavens, even the work of Thy fingers; * the moon and the stars which Thou hast ordained;
4 What is man, that Thou art mindful of him? * and the son of man, that Thou visitest him?
5 Thou madest him lower than the angels, * to crown him with glory and worship.
6 Thou makest him to have dominion of the works of Thy hands; * and Thou hast put all things in subjection under his feet:
7 All sheep and oxen; * yea, and the beasts of the field;
8 The fowls of the air, and the fishes of the sea; * and whatsoever walketh through the paths of the seas.
9 O Lord our Governor, * how excellent is Thy Name in all the world!

Second Day

Morning Prayer

Confitebor tibi   Psalm 9

1 I will give thanks unto Thee, O Lord, with my whole heart; * I will speak of all Thy marvelous works.
2 I will be glad and rejoice in Thee; * yea, my songs will I make of Thy Name, O Thou Most Highest.
3 While mine enemies are driven back, * they shall fall and perish at Thy presence.
4 For Thou hast maintained my right and my cause; * Thou art set in the throne that judgest right.
5 Thou hast rebuked the heathen, and destroyed the ungodly; * Thou hast put out their name for ever and ever.
6 O thou enemy, thy destructions are come to a perpetual end; * even as the cities which thou hast destroyed, whose memorial is perished with them.
7 But the Lord shall endure for ever; * He hath also prepared His seat for judgment.
8 For He shall judge the world in righteousness, * and minister true judgment unto the people.
9 The Lord also will be a defense for the oppressed, * even a refuge in due time of trouble.
10 And they that know Thy Name will put their trust in Thee; * for Thou, Lord, hast never failed them that seek Thee.
11 O praise the Lord Which dwelleth in Zion; * show the people of His doings.
12 For when He maketh inquisition for blood, He remembereth them, * and forgetteth not the complaint of the poor.
13 Have mercy upon me, O Lord; consider the trouble which I suffer of them that hate me, * Thou that liftest me up from the gates of death;
14 That I may show all Thy praises within the gates of the daughter of Zion: * I will rejoice in Thy salvation.

46

15 The heathen are sunk down in the pit that they made; * in the same net which they hid privily is their foot taken.
16 The Lord is known to execute judgment; * the ungodly is trapped in the work of his own hands.
17 The wicked shall be turned to destruction, * and all the people that forget God.
18 For the poor shall not alway be forgotten; * the patient abiding of the meek shall not perish for ever.
19 Up, Lord, and let not man have the upper hand; * let the heathen be judged in Thy sight.
20 Put them in fear, O Lord, * that the heathen may know themselves to be but men.

Ut quid, Domine?   Psalm 10

1 Why standest Thou so far off, O Lord, * and hidest Thy face in the needful time of trouble?
2 The ungodly, for his own lust, doth persecute the poor: * let them be taken in the crafty wiliness that they have imagined.
3 For the ungodly hath made boast of his own heart's desire, * and speaketh good of the covetous, whom the Lord abhorreth.
4 The ungodly is so proud, that he careth not for God, * neither is God in all his thoughts.
5 His ways are alway grievous; * Thy judgments are far above out of his sight, and therefore defieth he all his enemies.
6 For he hath said in his heart, "Tush, I shall never be cast down, * there shall no harm happen unto me."
7 His mouth is full of cursing, deceit, and fraud; * under his tongue is ungodliness and vanity.
8 He sitteth lurking in the thievish corners of the streets, * and privily in his lurking dens doth he murder the innocent; his eyes are set against the poor.
9 For he lieth waiting secretly; even as a lion lurketh he in his den, * that he may ravish the poor.

47

10 He doth ravish the poor, * when he getteth him into his net.
11 He falleth down, and humbleth himself, * that the congregation of the poor may fall into the hands of his captains.
12 He hath said in his heart, "Tush, God hath forgotten; * He hideth away His face, and He will never see it."
13 Arise, O Lord God, and lift up Thine hand; * forget not the poor.
14 Wherefore should the wicked blaspheme God, * while he doth say in his heart, "Tush, Thou God carest not for it?"
15 Surely Thou hast seen it; * for Thou beholdest ungodliness and wrong, that Thou mayest take the matter into Thy hand.
16 The poor committeth himself unto Thee; * for Thou art the helper of the friendless.
17 Break Thou the power of the ungodly and malicious; * search out his ungodliness, until Thou find none.
18 The Lord is King for ever and ever, * and the heathen are perished out of the land.
19 Lord, Thou hast heard the desire of the poor; * Thou preparest their heart, and Thine ear hearkeneth;
20 To help the fatherless and poor unto their right, * that the man of the earth be no more exalted against them.

In Domino confido   Psalm 11

1 In the Lord put I my trust; * how say ye then to my soul, "Flee as a bird unto the hill"?
2 For lo, the ungodly bend their bow, and make ready their arrows within the quiver, * that they may privily shoot at them which are true of heart.
3 If the foundations be destroyed, * what can the righteous do?
4 The Lord is in His holy temple; * the Lord's seat is in heaven.
5 His eyes consider the poor, * and His eyelids try the

children of men.

6 The Lord approveth the righteous: * but the ungodly, and him that delighteth in wickedness, doth His soul abhor.

7 Upon the ungodly He shall rain snares, fire and brimstone, storm and tempest: * this shall be their portion to drink.

8 For the righteous Lord loveth righteousness; * His countenance will behold the thing that is just.

Evening Prayer

Salvum me fac   Psalm 12

1 Help me, Lord, for there is not one godly man left; * for the faithful are minished from among the children of men.

2 They talk of vanity every one with his neighbor; * they do but flatter with their lips, and dissemble in their double heart.

3 The Lord shall root out all deceitful lips, * and the tongue that speaketh proud things;

4 Which have said, "With our tongue will we prevail; * we are they that ought to speak; who is lord over us?"

5 "Now, for the comfortless troubles' sake of the needy, * and because of the deep sighing of the poor,

6 I will up," saith the Lord; * "and will help every one from him that swelleth against him, and will set him at rest."

7 The words of the Lord are pure words; * even as the silver which from the earth is tried, and purified seven times in the fire.

8 Thou shalt keep them, O Lord; * Thou shalt preserve them from this generation for ever.

9 The ungodly walk on every side: * when they are exalted, the children of men are put to rebuke.

Usquequo, Domine?   Psalm 13

1 How long wilt Thou forget me, O Lord; for ever? * how long wilt Thou hide Thy face from me?
2 How long shall I seek counsel in my soul, and be so vexed in my heart? * how long shall mine enemy triumph over me?
3 Consider, and hear me, O Lord my God; * lighten mine eyes, that I sleep not in death;
4 Lest mine enemy say, "I have prevailed against him": * for if I be cast down, they that trouble me will rejoice at it.
5 But my trust is in Thy mercy, * and my heart is joyful in Thy salvation.
6 I will sing of the Lord, because He hath dealt so lovingly with me; * yea, I will praise the Name of the Lord Most Highest.

Dixit insipiens   Psalm 14

1 The fool hath said in his heart, * "There is no God."
2 They are corrupt, and become abominable in their doings; * there is none that doeth good, no not one.
3 The Lord looked down from heaven upon the children of men, * to see if there were any that would understand, and seek after God.
4 But they are all gone out of the way, they are altogether become abominable; * there is none that doeth good, no not one.
5 Have they no knowledge, that they are all such workers of mischief, * eating up my people as it were bread, and call not upon the Lord?
6 There were they brought in great fear, even where no fear was; * for God is in the generation of the righteous.
7 As for you, ye have made a mock at the counsel of the poor; * because he putteth his trust in the Lord.
8 Who shall give salvation unto Israel out of Zion? * When the Lord turneth the captivity of His people, then shall Jacob rejoice, and Israel shall be glad.

Third Day

Morning Prayer

Domine, quis habitabit?   Psalm 15

1 Lord, who shall dwell in Thy tabernacle? * or who shall rest upon Thy holy hill?
2 Even he that leadeth an incorrupt life, * and doeth the thing which is right, and speaketh the truth from his heart.
3 He that hath used no deceit in his tongue, nor done evil to his neighbor, * and hath not slandered his neighbor.
4 He that setteth not by himself, but is lowly in his own eyes, * and maketh much of them that fear the Lord.
5 He that sweareth unto his neighbor, and disappointeth him not, * though it were to his own hindrance.
6 He that hath not given his money upon usury, * nor taken reward against the innocent.
7 Whoso doeth these things * shall never fall.

Conserva me, Domine   Psalm 16

1 Preserve me, O God; * for in Thee have I put my trust.
2 O my soul, thou hast said unto the Lord, * "Thou art my God; I have no good like unto Thee."
3 All my delight is upon the saints that are in the earth, * and upon such as excel in virtue.
4 But they that run after another god * shall have great trouble.
5 Their drink-offerings of blood will I not offer, * neither make mention of their names within my lips.
6 The Lord Himself is the portion of mine inheritance, and of my cup; * Thou shalt maintain my lot.
7 The lot is fallen unto me in a fair ground; * yea, I have a goodly heritage.
8 I will thank the Lord for giving me warning; * my reins also chasten me in the night season.

9 I have set the Lord alway before me; * for He is on my right hand, therefore I shall not fall.
10 Wherefore my heart is glad, and my glory rejoiceth: * my flesh also shall rest in hope.
11 For why? Thou shalt not leave my soul in hell; * neither shalt Thou suffer Thy Holy One to see corruption.
12 Thou shalt show me the path of life: in Thy presence is the fullness of joy, * and at Thy right hand there is pleasure for evermore.

Exaudi, Domine   Psalm 17

1 Hear the right, O Lord, consider my complaint, * and hearken unto my prayer, that goeth not out of feigned lips.
2 Let my sentence come forth from Thy presence; * and let Thine eyes look upon the thing that is equal.
3 Thou hast proved and visited mine heart in the night season; Thou hast tried me, and shalt find no wickedness in me; * for I am utterly purposed that my mouth shall not offend.
4 As for the works of men, * by the word of Thy lips I have kept me from the ways of the destroyer.
5 O hold Thou up my goings in Thy paths, * that my footsteps slip not.
6 I have called upon Thee, O God, for Thou shalt hear me: * incline Thine ear to me, and hearken unto my words.
7 Show Thy marvelous loving-kindness, Thou that art the Savior of them which put their trust in Thee, * from such as resist Thy right hand.
8 Keep me as the apple of an eye; * hide me under the shadow of Thy wings,
9 From the ungodly, that trouble me; * mine enemies compass me round about, to take away my soul.
10 They are enclosed in their own fat, * and their mouth speaketh proud things.
11 They lie waiting in our way on every side, * watching to cast us down to the ground;

12 Like as a lion that is greedy of his prey, * and as it were a lion's whelp lurking in secret places.
13 Up, Lord, disappoint him, and cast him down; * deliver my soul from the ungodly, by Thine own sword;
14 Yea, by Thy hand, O Lord; from the men of the evil world; * which have their portion in this life, whose bellies Thou fillest with Thy hid treasure.
15 They have children at their desire, * and leave the rest of their substance for their babes.
16 But as for me, I shall behold Thy presence in righteousness; * and when I awake up after Thy likeness, I shall be satisfied.

Evening Prayer

Diligam te, Domine   Psalm 18

1 "I will love Thee, O Lord, my strength. * The Lord is my stony rock, and my defense;
2 My Savior, my God, and my might, in Whom I will trust; * my buckler, the horn also of my salvation, and my refuge.
3 I will call upon the Lord, Which is worthy to be praised; * so shall I be safe from mine enemies.
4 The sorrows of death compassed me, * and the overflowings of ungodliness made me afraid.
5 The pains of hell came about me; * the snares of death overtook me.
6 In my trouble I called upon the Lord, * and complained unto my God:
7 So He heard my voice out of His holy temple, * and my complaint came before Him; it entered even into His ears.
8 The earth trembled and quaked, * the very foundations also of the hills shook, and were removed, because He was wroth.
9 There went a smoke out in His presence, * and a consuming fire out of His mouth, so that coals were kindled at it.

10 He bowed the heavens also, and came down, * and it was dark under His feet.
11 He rode upon the Cherubim, and did fly; * He came flying upon the wings of the wind.
12 He made darkness His secret place, * His pavilion round about Him with dark water, and thick clouds to cover Him.
13 At the brightness of His presence His clouds removed; * hailstones and coals of fire.
14 The Lord also thundered out of heaven, and the Highest gave His thunder; * hailstones and coals of fire.
15 He sent out His arrows, and scattered them; * He cast forth lightnings, and destroyed them.
16 The springs of waters were seen, and the foundations of the round world were discovered, * at Thy chiding, O Lord, at the blasting of the breath of Thy displeasure.
17 He sent down from on high to fetch me, * and took me out of many waters.
18 He delivered me from my strongest enemy, and from them which hate me; * for they were too mighty for me.
19 They came upon me in the day of my trouble; * but the Lord was my upholder.
20 He brought me forth also into a place of liberty; * He brought me forth, even because He had a favor unto me.
21 The Lord rewarded me after my righteous dealing, * according to the cleanness of my hands did He recompense me.
22 Because I have kept the ways of the Lord, * and have not forsaken my God, as the wicked doth.
23 For I have an eye unto all His laws, * and will not cast out His commandments from me.
24 I was also incorrupt before Him, * and eschewed mine own wickedness.
25 Therefore the Lord rewarded me after my righteous dealing, * and according unto the cleanness of my hands in His eyesight.
26 With the holy Thou shalt be holy, * and with a perfect man Thou shalt be perfect.

27 With the clean Thou shalt be clean, * and with the froward Thou shalt be froward.

28 For Thou shalt save the people that are in adversity, and shalt bring down the high looks of the proud.

29 Thou also shalt light my candle; * the Lord my God shall make my darkness to be light.

30 For in Thee I shall discomfit an host of men, * and with the help of my God I shall leap over the wall.

31 The way of God is an undefiled way: * the word of the Lord also is tried in the fire; He is the defender of all them that put their trust in Him.

32 For who is God, but the Lord? * or who hath any strength, except our God?

33 It is God that girdeth me with strength of war, * and maketh my way perfect.

34 He maketh my feet like harts' feet, * and setteth me up on high.

35 He teacheth mine hands to fight, * and mine arms shall bend even a bow of steel.

36 Thou hast given me the defense of Thy salvation; * Thy right hand also shall hold me up, and Thy loving correction shall make me great.

37 Thou shalt make room enough under me for to go, * that my footsteps shall not slide.

38 I will follow upon mine enemies, and overtake them; * neither will I turn again till I have destroyed them.

39 I will smite them, that they shall not be able to stand, * but fall under my feet.

40 Thou hast girded me with strength unto the battle; * Thou shalt throw down mine enemies under me.

41 Thou hast made mine enemies also to turn their backs upon me, * and I shall destroy them that hate me.

42 They shall cry, but there shall be none to help them; * yea, even unto the Lord shall they cry, but He shall not hear them.

43 I will beat them as small as the dust before the wind: * I will cast them out as the clay in the streets.

44 Thou shalt deliver me from the strivings of the people, * and Thou shalt make me the head of the nations; a people whom I have not known shall serve me.

45 As soon as they hear of me, they shall obey me; * the strangers shall feign obedience unto me.

46 The strangers shall fail, * and come trembling out of their strongholds.

47 The Lord liveth; and blessed be my strong helper, * and praised be the God of my salvation;

48 Even the God that seeth that I be avenged, * and subdueth the people unto me.

49 It is He that delivereth me from my cruel enemies, and setteth me up above mine adversaries: * Thou shalt rid me from the wicked man.

50 For this cause will I give thanks unto Thee, O Lord, among the Gentiles, * and sing praises unto Thy Name.

51 Great prosperity giveth He unto His king, * and showeth loving-kindness unto His Anointed, unto David and his seed for evermore."

Fourth Day

Morning Prayer

Caeli enarrant   Psalm 19

1 The heavens declare the glory of God; * and the firmament showeth His handy-work.

2 One day telleth another; * and one night certifieth another.

3 There is neither speech nor language; * but their voices are heard among them.

4 Their sound is gone out into all lands; * and their words into the ends of the world.

5 In them hath He set a tabernacle for the sun; * which cometh forth as a bridegroom out of his chamber, and rejoiceth as a giant to run his course.

6 It goeth forth from the uttermost part of the heaven, and

runneth about unto the end of it again; * and there is
nothing hid from the heat thereof.
7 The law of the Lord is an undefiled law, converting the
soul; * the testimony of the Lord is sure, and giveth wisdom
unto the simple.
8 The statutes of the Lord are right, and rejoice the heart; *
the commandment of the Lord is pure, and giveth light unto
the eyes.
9 The fear of the Lord is clean, and endureth for ever; * the
judgments of the Lord are true, and righteous altogether.
10 More to be desired are they than gold, yea, than much
fine gold; * sweeter also than honey, and the honeycomb.
11 Moreover, by them is Thy servant taught; * and in
keeping of them there is great reward.
12 Who can tell how oft he offendeth? * O cleanse Thou me
from my secret faults.
13 Keep Thy servant also from presumptuous sins, lest
they get the dominion over me; * so shall I be undefiled,
and innocent from the great offense.
14 Let the words of my mouth, and the meditation of my
heart, be alway acceptable in Thy sight, * O Lord, my
strength and my redeemer.

Exaudiat te Dominus   Psalm 20

1 The Lord hear thee in the day of trouble; * the Name of
the God of Jacob defend thee:
2 Send thee help from the sanctuary, * and strengthen thee
out of Zion:
3 Remember all thy offerings, * and accept thy burnt-
sacrifice:
4 Grant thee thy heart's desire, * and fulfill all thy mind.
5 We will rejoice in Thy salvation, and triumph in the Name
of the Lord our God: * the Lord perform all thy petitions.
6 Now know I that the Lord helpeth His Anointed, and will
hear Him from His holy heaven, * even with the wholesome
strength of His right hand.

7 Some put their trust in chariots, and some in horses; * but we will remember the Name of the Lord our God.
8 They are brought down and fallen; * but we are risen and stand upright.
9 Save Thy King, O Lord; * and hear us when we call upon Thee.

Domine, in virtute tua   Psalm 21

1 The king shall rejoice in Thy strength, O Lord; * exceeding glad shall he be of Thy salvation.
2 Thou hast given him his heart's desire, * and hast not denied him the request of his lips.
3 For Thou shalt meet him with the blessings of goodness, * and shalt set a crown of pure gold upon his head.
4 He asked life of Thee; and Thou gavest him a long life, * even for ever and ever.
5 His honor is great in Thy salvation; * glory and great worship shalt Thou lay upon him.
6 For Thou shalt give him everlasting felicity, * and make him glad with the joy of Thy countenance.
7 And why? because the King putteth his trust in the Lord; * and in the mercy of the Most Highest he shall not miscarry.
8 All Thine enemies shall feel Thine hand; * Thy right hand shall find out them that hate Thee.
9 Thou shalt make them like a fiery oven in time of Thy wrath: * the Lord shall destroy them in His displeasure, and the fire shall consume them.
10 Their fruit shalt Thou root out of the earth, * and their seed from among the children of men.
11 For they intended mischief against Thee, * and imagined such a device as they are not able to perform.
12 Therefore shalt Thou put them to flight, * and the strings of Thy bow shalt Thou make ready against the face of them.
13 Be Thou exalted, Lord, in Thine own strength; * so will we sing, and praise Thy power.

58

Evening Prayer

Deus, Deus meus   Psalm 22

1 My God, my God, look upon me; why hast Thou forsaken me? * and art so far from my health, and from the words of my complaint?

2 O My God, I cry in the day-time, but Thou hearest not; * and in the night season also I take no rest.

3 And Thou continuest holy, * O Thou Worship of Israel.

4 Our fathers hoped in Thee; * they trusted in Thee, and Thou didst deliver them.

5 They called upon Thee, and were holpen; * they put their trust in Thee, and were not confounded.

6 But as for me, I am a worm, and no man; * a very scorn of men, and the outcast of the people.

7 All they that see me laugh me to scorn; * they shoot out their lips, and shake their heads, saying,

8 "He trusted in the Lord, that He would deliver him; * let Him deliver him, if He will have him."

9 But Thou art He that took me out of my mother's womb; * Thou wast my hope, when I hanged yet upon My mother's breasts.

10 I have been left unto Thee ever since I was born; * Thou art my God even from my mother's womb.

11 O go not from Me; for trouble is hard at hand, * and there is none to help me.

12 Many oxen are come about me; * fat bulls of Bashan close me in on every side.

13 They gape upon me with their mouths, * as it were a ramping and a roaring lion.

14 I am poured out like water, and all my bones are out of joint; * my heart also in the midst of my body is even like melting wax.

15 My strength is dried up like a potsherd, and my tongue cleaveth to my gums, * and Thou bringest me into the dust of death.

59

16 For many dogs are come about me, * and the council of the wicked layeth siege against me.
17 They pierced my hands and my feet: I may tell all my bones: * they stand staring and looking upon me.
18 They part my garments among them, * and cast lots upon my vesture.
19 But be not Thou far from me, O Lord; * Thou art my succor, haste Thee to help me.
20 Deliver my soul from the sword, * my darling from the power of the dog.
21 Save me from the lion's mouth; * Thou hast heard me also from among the horns of the unicorns.
22 I will declare Thy Name unto my brethren; * in the midst of the congregation will I praise Thee.
23 O praise the Lord, ye that fear Him: * magnify Him, all ye of the seed of Jacob; and fear Him, all ye seed of Israel.
24 For He hath not despised nor abhorred the low estate of the poor; * He hath not hid His face from him; but when he called unto Him He heard him.
25 My praise is of Thee in the great-congregation; * my vows will I perform in the sight of them that fear Him.
26 The poor shall eat, and be satisfied; they that seek after the Lord shall praise Him: * their heart shall live for ever.
27 All the ends of the world shall remember themselves, and be turned unto the Lord; * and all the kindreds of the nations shall worship before Him.
28 For the Kingdom is the Lord's, * and He is the Governor among the nations.
29 All such as be fat upon earth * have eaten, and worshiped.
30 All they that go down into the dust shall kneel before Him; * and no man hath quickened his own soul.
31 My seed shall serve Him: * they shall be counted unto the Lord for a generation.
32 They shall come, and shall declare His righteousness * unto a people that shall be born, whom the Lord hath made.

Dominus regit me   Psalm 23

1 The Lord is my shepherd; * I shall not want.
2 He maketh me to lie down in green pastures: * He leadeth me beside the still waters.
3 He restoreth my soul: * He leadeth me in the paths of righteousness for His Name's sake.
4 Yea, though I walk through the valley of the shadow of death, I will fear no evil: * for Thou art with me; Thy rod and Thy staff they comfort me.
5 Thou preparest a table before me in the presence of mine enemies: * Thou anointest my head with oil; my cup runneth over.
6 Surely goodness and mercy shall follow me all the days of my life: * and I will dwell in the house of the Lord for ever.

Fifth Day

Morning Prayer

Domini est terra   Psalm 24

1 The earth is the Lord's, and all that therein is; * the compass of the world, and they that dwell therein.
2 For He hath founded it upon the seas, * and established it upon the floods.
3 Who shall ascend into the hill of the Lord? * or who shall rise up in His holy place?
4 Even he that hath clean hands, and a pure heart; * and that hath not lift up his mind unto vanity, nor sworn to deceive his neighbor.
5 He shall receive the blessing from the Lord, * and righteousness from the God of his salvation.
6 This is the generation of them that seek Him; * even of them that seek Thy face, O God of Jacob.
7 Lift up your heads, O ye gates; and be ye lift up, ye everlasting doors; * and the King of glory shall come in.

8 Who is this King of glory? * It is the Lord strong and mighty, even the Lord mighty in battle.
9 Lift up your heads, O ye gates; and be ye lift up, ye everlasting doors; * and the King of glory shall come in.
10 Who is this King of glory? * Even the Lord of hosts, He is the King of glory.

Ad te, Domine, levavi　　　　　　　　　Psalm 25

1 Unto Thee, O Lord, will I lift up my soul; my God, I have put my trust in Thee: * O let me not be confounded, neither let mine enemies triumph over me.
2 For all they that hope in Thee shall not be ashamed; * but such as transgress without a cause shall be put to confusion.
3 Show me Thy ways, O Lord, * and teach me Thy paths.
4 Lead me forth in Thy truth, and learn me: * for Thou art the God of my salvation; in Thee hath been my hope all the day long.
5 Call to remembrance, O Lord, Thy tender mercies, * and Thy loving-kindnesses, which have been ever of old.
6 O remember not the sins and offenses of my youth; * but according to Thy mercy think Thou upon me, O Lord, for Thy goodness.
7 Gracious and righteous is the Lord; * therefore, will He teach sinners in the way.
8 Them that are meek shall He guide in judgment; * and such as are gentle, them shall He learn His way.
9 All the paths of the Lord are mercy and truth, * unto such as keep His covenant and His testimonies.
10 For Thy Name's sake, O Lord, * be merciful unto my sin; for it is great.
11 What man is he that feareth the Lord? * him shall He teach in the way that He shall choose.
12 His soul shall dwell at ease, * and his seed shall inherit the land.

13 The secret of the Lord is among them that fear Him; *
and He will show them His covenant.
14 Mine eyes are ever looking unto the Lord; * for He shall
pluck my feet out of the net.
15 Turn Thee unto me, and have mercy upon me; * for I am
desolate, and in misery.
16 The sorrows of my heart are enlarged: * O bring Thou
me out of my troubles.
17 Look upon my adversity and misery, * and forgive me all
my sin.
18 Consider mine enemies, how many they are; * and they
bear a tyrannous hate against me.
19 O keep my soul, and deliver me: * let me not be
confounded, for I have put my trust in Thee.
20 Let perfectness and righteous dealing wait upon me; *
for my hope hath been in Thee.
21 Deliver Israel, O God, * out of all his troubles.

Judica me, Domine   Psalm 26

1 Be Thou my Judge, O Lord, for I have walked innocently:
* my trust hath been also in the Lord, therefore shall I not
fall.
2 Examine me, O Lord, and prove me; * try out my reins
and my heart.
3 For Thy loving-kindness is ever before mine eyes; * and I
will walk in Thy truth.
4 I have not dwelt with vain persons; * neither will I have
fellowship with the deceitful.
5 I have hated the congregation of the wicked; * and will not
sit among the ungodly.
6 I will wash my hands in innocence, O Lord; * and so will I
go to Thine altar;
7 That I may show the voice of thanksgiving, * and tell of all
Thy wondrous works.
8 Lord, I have loved the habitation of Thy house, * and the
place where Thine honor dwelleth.

9 O shut not up my soul with the sinners, * nor my life with the blood-thirsty;

10 In whose hands is wickedness, * and their right hand is full of gifts.

11 But as for me, I will walk innocently: * O deliver me, and be merciful unto me.

12 My foot standeth right: * I will praise the Lord in the congregations.

Evening Prayer

Dominus illuminatio   Psalm 27

1 The Lord is my light and my salvation; whom then shall I fear? * the Lord is the strength of my life; of whom then shall I be afraid?

2 When the wicked, even mine enemies and my foes, came upon me to eat up my flesh, * they stumbled and fell.

3 Though an host of men were laid against me, yet shall not my heart be afraid; * and though there rose up war against me, yet will I put my trust in Him.

4 One thing have I desired of the Lord, which I will require; * even that I may dwell in the house of the Lord all the days of my life, to behold the fair beauty of the Lord, and to visit His temple.

5 For in the time of trouble He shall hide me in His tabernacle; * yea, in the secret place of His dwelling shall He hide me, and set me up upon a rock of stone.

6 And now shall He lift up mine head * above mine enemies round about me.

7 Therefore will I offer in His dwelling an oblation, with great gladness: * I will sing and speak praises unto the Lord.

8 Hearken unto my voice, O Lord, when I cry unto Thee; * have mercy upon me, and hear me.

9 My heart hath talked of Thee, "Seek ye my face": * "Thy face, Lord, will I seek."

10 O hide not Thou Thy face from me, * nor cast Thy servant away in displeasure.

11 Thou hast been my succor; * leave me not, neither forsake me, O God of my salvation.

12 When my father and my mother forsake me, * the Lord taketh me up.

13 Teach me Thy way, O Lord, * and lead me in the right way, because of mine enemies.

14 Deliver me not over into the will of mine adversaries: * for there are false witnesses risen up against me, and such as speak wrong.

15 I should utterly have fainted, * but that I believe verily to see the goodness of the Lord in the land of the living.

16 O tarry thou the Lord's leisure; * be strong, and He shall comfort thine heart; and put thou thy trust in the Lord.

Ad te, Domine   Psalm 28

1 Unto Thee will I cry, O Lord, my strength: * think no scorn of me; lest, if Thou make as though Thou hearest not, I become like them that go down into the pit.

2 Hear the voice of my humble petitions, when I cry unto Thee; * when I hold up my hands towards the mercyseat of Thy holy temple.

3 O pluck me not away, neither destroy me with the ungodly and wicked doers, * which speak friendly to their neighbors, but imagine mischief in their hearts.

4 Reward them according to their deeds, * and according to the wickedness of their own inventions.

5 Recompense them after the work of their hands; * pay them that they have deserved.

6 For they regard not in their mind the works of the Lord, nor the operation of His hands; * therefore shall He break them down, and not build them up.

7 Praised be the Lord; * for He hath heard the voice of my humble petitions.

8 The Lord is my strength, and my shield; my heart hath trusted in Him, and I am helped; * therefore my heart danceth for joy, and in my song will I praise Him.
9 The Lord is my strength, * and He is the wholesome defense of His anointed.
10 O save Thy people, and give Thy blessing unto Thine inheritance: * feed them, and set them up for ever.

Afferte Domino   Psalm 29

1 Ascribe unto the Lord, O ye mighty, * ascribe unto the Lord worship and strength.
2 Ascribe unto the Lord the honor due unto His Name; * worship the Lord with holy worship.
3 The voice of the Lord is upon the waters; * it is the glorious God that maketh the thunder.
4 It is the Lord that ruleth the sea; the voice of the Lord is mighty in operation; * the voice of the Lord is a glorious voice.
5 The voice of the Lord breaketh the cedar-trees; * yea, the Lord breaketh the cedars of Lebanon.
6 He maketh them also to skip like a calf; * Lebanon also, and Sirion, like a young unicorn.
7 The voice of the Lord divideth the flames of fire; the voice of the Lord shaketh the wilderness; * yea, the Lord shaketh the wilderness of Kadesh.
8 The voice of the Lord maketh the hinds to bring forth young, and strippeth bare the forests: * in His temple doth every thing speak of His honor.
9 The Lord sitteth above the water-flood, * and the Lord remaineth a King for ever.
10 The Lord shall give strength unto His people; * the Lord shall give His people the blessing of peace.

Sixth Day

Morning Prayer

Exaltabo te, Domine   Psalm 30

1 I will magnify Thee, O Lord; for Thou hast set me up, *
and not made my foes to triumph over me.
2 O Lord my God, I cried unto Thee; * and Thou hast
healed me.
3 Thou, Lord, hast brought my soul out of hell: * Thou hast
kept my life, that I should not go down into the pit.
4 Sing praises unto the Lord, O ye saints of His; * and give
thanks unto Him, for a remembrance of His holiness.
5 For His wrath endureth but the twinkling of an eye, and in
His pleasure is life; * heaviness may endure for a night, but
joy cometh in the morning.
6 And in my prosperity I said, "I shall never be removed": *
Thou, Lord, of Thy goodness, hast made my hill so strong.
7 Thou didst turn Thy face from me, * and I was troubled.
8 Then cried I unto Thee, O Lord; * and gat me to my Lord
right humbly.
9 "What profit is there in my blood, * when I go down into
the pit?
10 Shall the dust give thanks unto Thee? * or shall it
declare Thy truth?
11 Hear, O Lord, and have mercy upon me; * Lord, be Thou
my helper."
12 Thou hast turned my heaviness into joy; * Thou hast put
off my sackcloth, and girded me with gladness:
13 Therefore shall every good man sing of Thy praise
without ceasing. * O my God, I will give thanks unto Thee
for ever.

1 In Thee, O Lord, have I put my trust; let me never be put to confusion; * deliver me in Thy righteousness.
2 Bow down Thine ear to me; * make haste to deliver me.
3 And be Thou my strong rock, and house of defense, * that Thou mayest save me.
4 For Thou art my strong rock, and my castle: * be Thou also my guide, and lead me for Thy Name's sake.
5 Draw me out of the net that they have laid privily for me; * for Thou art my strength.
6 Into Thy hands I commend my spirit; * for Thou hast redeemed me, O Lord, Thou God of truth.
7 I have hated them that hold of lying vanities, * and my trust hath been in the Lord.
8 I will be glad and rejoice in Thy mercy; * for Thou hast considered my trouble, and hast known my soul in adversities.
9 Thou hast not shut me up into the hand of the enemy; * but hast set my feet in a large room.
10 Have mercy upon me, O Lord, for I am in trouble, * and mine eye is consumed for very heaviness; yea, my soul and my body.
11 For my life is waxen old with heaviness, * and my years with mourning.
12 My strength faileth me, because of mine iniquity, * and my bones are consumed.
13 I became a reproach among all mine enemies, but especially among my neighbors; * and they of mine acquaintance were afraid of me; and they that did see me without, conveyed themselves from me.
14 I am clean forgotten as a dead man out of mind; * I am become like a broken vessel.
15 For I have heard the blasphemy of the multitude, and fear is on every side; * while they conspire together against me, and take their counsel to take away my life.
16 But my hope hath been in Thee, O Lord; * I have said,

"Thou art my God."
17 My times are in Thy hand; deliver me from the hand of mine enemies, * and from them that persecute me.
18 Show Thy servant the light of Thy countenance, * and save me for Thy mercy's sake.
19 Let me not be confounded, O Lord, for I have called upon Thee; * let the ungodly be put to confusion, and be put to silence in the grave.
20 Let the lying lips be put to silence, * which cruelly, disdainfully, and despitefully speak against the righteous.
21 O how plentiful is Thy goodness, which Thou hast laid up for them that fear Thee, * and that Thou hast prepared for them that put their trust in Thee, even before the sons of men!
22 Thou shalt hide them in the covert of Thine own presence from the plottings of men: * Thou shalt keep them secretly in Thy tabernacle from the strife of tongues.
23 Thanks be to the Lord; * for He hath showed me marvelous great kindness in a strong city.
24 But in my haste I said, * "I am cast out of the sight of Thine eyes."
25 Nevertheless, Thou heardest the voice of my prayer, * when I cried unto Thee.
26 O love the Lord, all ye His saints; * for the Lord preserveth them that are faithful, and plenteously rewardeth the proud doer.
27 Be strong, and He shall establish your heart, * all ye that put your trust in the Lord.

Evening Prayer

Beati quorum   Psalm 32

1 Blessed is he whose unrighteousness is forgiven, * and whose sin is covered.
2 Blessed is the man unto whom the Lord imputeth no sin, * and in whose spirit there is no guile.

3 For whilst I held my tongue, * my bones consumed away through my daily complaining.
4 For Thy hand was heavy upon me day and night, * and my moisture was like the drought in summer.
5 I acknowledged my sin unto Thee; * and mine unrighteousness have I not hid.
6 I said, "I will confess my sins unto the Lord"; * and so Thou forgavest the wickedness of my sin.
7 For this shall every one that is godly make his prayer unto Thee, in a time when Thou mayest be found; * surely the great water-floods shall not come nigh him.
8 Thou art a place to hide me in; Thou shalt preserve me from trouble; * Thou shalt compass me about with songs of deliverance.
9 "I will inform thee, and teach thee in the way wherein thou shalt go; * and I will guide thee with Mine eye.
10 Be ye not like to horse and mule, which have no understanding; * whose mouths must be held with bit and bridle, else they will not obey thee."
11 Great plagues remain for the ungodly; * but whoso putteth his trust in the Lord, mercy embraceth him on every side.
12 Be glad, O ye righteous, and rejoice in the Lord; * and be joyful, all ye that are true of heart.

Exultate, justi   Psalm 33

1 Rejoice in the Lord, O ye righteous; * for it becometh well the just to be thankful.
2 Praise the Lord with harp; * sing praises unto Him with the lute, and instrument of ten strings.
3 Sing unto the Lord a new song; * sing praises lustily unto Him with a good courage.
4 For the word of the Lord is true; * and all His works are faithful.
5 He loveth righteousness and judgment; * the earth is full of the goodness of the Lord.

6 By the word of the Lord were the heavens made; * and all the host of them by the breath of His mouth.

7 He gathereth the waters of the sea together, as it were upon an heap; * and layeth up the deep, as in a treasure-house.

8 Let all the earth fear the Lord: * stand in awe of Him, all ye that dwell in the world.

9 For He spake, and it was done; * He commanded, and it stood fast.

10 The Lord bringeth the counsel of the heathen to naught, * and maketh the devices of the people to be of none effect, and casteth out the counsels of princes.

11 The counsel of the Lord shall endure for ever, * and the thoughts of His heart from generation to generation.

12 Blessed are the people whose God is the Lord Jehovah; * and blessed are the folk that He hath chosen to Him, to be His inheritance.

13 The Lord looketh down from heaven, and beholdeth all the children of men; * from the habitation of His dwelling, He considereth all them that dwell on the earth.

14 He fashioneth all the hearts of them, * and understandeth all their works.

15 There is no king that can be saved by the multitude of an host; * neither is any mighty man delivered by much strength.

16 A horse is counted but a vain thing to save a man; * neither shall he deliver any man by his great strength.

17 Behold, the eye of the Lord is upon them that fear Him, * and upon them that put their trust in His mercy;

18 To deliver their soul from death, * and to feed them in the time of dearth.

19 Our soul hath patiently tarried for the Lord; * for He is our help and our shield.

20 For our heart shall rejoice in Him; * because we have hoped in His holy Name.

21 Let Thy merciful kindness, O Lord, be upon us, * like as we do put our trust in Thee.

1 I will alway give thanks unto the Lord; * His praise shall ever be in my mouth.
2 My soul shall make her boast in the Lord; * the humble shall hear thereof, and be glad.
3 O praise the Lord with me, * and let us magnify His Name together.
4 I sought the Lord, and He heard me; * yea, He delivered me out of all my fear.
5 They had an eye unto Him, and were lightened; * and their faces were not ashamed.
6 Lo, the poor crieth, and the Lord heareth him; * yea, and saveth him out of all his troubles.
7 The angel of the Lord tarrieth round about them that fear Him, * and delivereth them.
8 O taste, and see, how gracious the Lord is: * blessed is the man that trusteth in Him.
9 O fear the Lord, ye that are His saints; * for they that fear Him lack nothing.
10 The lions do lack, and suffer hunger; * but they who seek the Lord shall want no manner of thing that is good.
11 Come, ye children, and hearken unto me; * I will teach you the fear of the Lord.
12 What man is he that lusteth to live, * and would fain see good days?
13 Keep thy tongue from evil, * and thy lips, that they speak no guile.
14 Eschew evil, and do good; * seek peace, and ensue it.
15 The eyes of the Lord are over the righteous, * and His ears are open unto their prayers.
16 The countenance of the Lord is against them that do evil, * to root out the remembrance of them from the earth.
17 The righteous cry, and the Lord heareth them, * and delivereth them out of all their troubles.
18 The Lord is nigh unto them that are of a contrite heart, *

and will save such as be of an humble spirit.
19 Great are the troubles of the righteous; * but the Lord delivereth him out of all.
20 He keepeth all his bones, * so that not one of them is broken.
21 But misfortune shall slay the ungodly; * and they that hate the righteous shall be desolate.
22 The Lord delivereth the souls of His servants; * and all they that put their trust in Him shall not be destitute.

Seventh Day

Morning Prayer

Judica, Domine   Psalm 35

1 Plead Thou my cause, O Lord, with them that strive with me, * and fight Thou against them that fight against me.
2 Lay hand upon the shield and buckler, * and stand up to help me.
3 Bring forth the spear, and stop the way against them that pursue me: * say unto my soul, "I am thy salvation."
4 Let them be confounded, and put to shame, that seek after my soul; * let them be turned back, and brought to confusion, that imagine mischief for me.
5 Let them be as the dust before the wind, * and the angel of the Lord scattering them.
6 Let their way be dark and slippery, * and let the angel of the Lord pursue them.
7 For they have privily laid their net to destroy me without a cause; * yea, even without a cause have they made a pit for my soul.
8 Let a sudden destruction come upon him unawares, and his net that he hath laid privily catch himself; * that he may fall into his own mischief.
9 And my soul shall be joyful in the Lord; * it shall rejoice in His salvation.

10 All my bones shall say, "Lord, who is like unto Thee, Who deliverest the poor from him that is too strong for him; * yea, the poor, and him that is in misery, from him that spoileth him?"
11 False witnesses did rise up: * they laid to my charge things that I knew not.
12 They rewarded me evil for good, * to the great discomfort of my soul.
13 Nevertheless, when they were sick, I put on sackcloth, and humbled my soul with fasting; * and my prayer shall turn into mine own bosom.
14 I behaved myself as though it had been my friend or my brother; * I went heavily, as one that mourneth for his mother.
15 But in mine adversity they rejoiced, and gathered themselves together; * yea, the very abjects came together against me unawares, making mouths at me, and ceased not.
16 With the flatterers were busy mockers, * who gnashed upon me with their teeth.
17 Lord, how long wilt Thou look upon this? * O deliver my soul from the calamities which they bring on me, and my darling from the lions.
18 So will I give Thee thanks in the great congregation; * I will praise Thee among much people.
19 O let not them that are mine enemies triumph over me ungodly; * neither let them wink with their eyes, that hate me without a cause.
20 And why? their communing is not for peace; * but they imagine deceitful words against them that are quiet in the land.
21 They gaped upon me with their mouths, and said, * "Fie on thee! fie on thee! we saw it with our eyes."
22 This Thou hast seen, O Lord; * hold not Thy tongue then; go not far from me, O Lord.
23 Awake, and stand up to judge my quarrel; * avenge Thou my cause, my God and my Lord.

24 Judge me, O Lord my God, according to Thy righteousness; * and let them not triumph over me.
25 Let them not say in their hearts, "There! there! so would we have it"; * neither let them say, "We have devoured him."
26 Let them be put to confusion and shame together, that rejoice at my trouble; * let them be clothed with rebuke and dishonor, that boast themselves against me.
27 Let them be glad and rejoice, that favor my righteous dealing; * yea, let them say alway, "Blessed be the Lord, Who hath pleasure in the prosperity of His servant."
28 And as for my tongue, it shall be talking of Thy righteousness, * and of Thy praise, all the day long.

Dixit injustus   Psalm 36

1 My heart showeth me the wickedness of the ungodly, * that there is no fear of God before his eyes.
2 For he flattereth himself in his own sight, * until his abominable sin be found out.
3 The words of his mouth are unrighteous and full of deceit: * he hath left off to behave himself wisely, and to do good.
4 He imagineth mischief upon his bed, and hath set himself in no good way; * neither doth he abhor any thing that is evil.
5 Thy mercy, O Lord, reacheth unto the heavens, * and Thy faithfulness unto the clouds.
6 Thy righteousness standeth like the strong mountains: * Thy judgments are like the great deep.
7 Thou, Lord, shalt save both man and beast: how excellent is Thy mercy, O God! * and the children of men shall put their trust under the shadow of Thy wings.
8 They shall be satisfied with the plenteousness of Thy house; * and Thou shalt give them drink of Thy pleasures, as out of the river.
9 For with Thee is the well of life; * and in Thy light shall we see light.

10 O continue forth Thy loving-kindness unto them that know Thee, * and Thy righteousness unto them that are true of heart.
11 O let not the foot of pride come against me; * and let not the hand of the ungodly cast me down.
12 There are they fallen, all that work wickedness; * they are cast down, and shall not be able to stand.

Evening Prayer

Noli aemulari   Psalm 37

1 Fret not thyself because of the ungodly; * neither be thou envious against the evil doers.
2 For they shall soon be cut down like the grass, * and be withered even as the green herb.
3 Put thou thy trust in the Lord, and be doing good; * dwell in the land, and verily thou shalt be fed.
4 Delight thou in the Lord, * and He shall give thee thy heart's desire.
5 Commit thy way unto the Lord, and put thy trust in Him, * and He shall bring it to pass.
6 He shall make thy righteousness as clear as the light, * and thy just dealing as the noon-day.
7 Hold thee still in the Lord, and abide patiently upon Him: * but grieve not thyself at Him Whose way doth prosper, against the man that doeth after evil counsels.
8 Leave off from wrath, and let go displeasure: * fret not thyself, else shalt thou be moved to do evil.
9 Wicked doers shall be rooted out; * and they that patiently abide the Lord, those shall inherit the land.
10 Yet a little while, and the ungodly shall be clean gone: * thou shalt look after his place, and he shall be away.
11 But the meek-spirited shall possess the earth, * and shall be refreshed in the multitude of peace.
12 The ungodly seeketh counsel against the just, * and gnasheth upon him with his teeth.

13 The Lord shall laugh him to-scorn; * for He hath seen that his day is coming.

14 The ungodly have drawn out the sword, and have bent their bow, * to cast down the poor and needy, and to slay such as be upright in their ways.

15 Their sword shall go through their own heart, * and their bow shall be broken.

16 A small thing that the righteous hath, * is better than great riches of the ungodly.

17 For the arms of the ungodly shall be broken, * and the Lord upholdeth the righteous.

18 The Lord knoweth the days of the godly; * and their inheritance shall endure for ever.

19 They shall not be confounded in the perilous time; * and in the days of dearth they shall have enough.

20 As for the ungodly, they shall perish, and the enemies of the Lord shall consume as the fat of lambs: * yea, even as the smoke shall they consume away.

21 The ungodly borroweth, and payeth not again; * but the righteous is merciful and liberal.

22 Such as are blessed of God, shall possess the land; * and they that are cursed of Him, shall be rooted out.

23 The Lord ordereth a good man's going, * and maketh his way acceptable to Himself.

24 Though he fall, he shall not be cast away; * for the Lord upholdeth him with His hand.

25 I have been young, and now am old; * and yet saw I never the righteous forsaken, nor his seed begging their bread.

26 The righteous is ever merciful, and lendeth; * and his seed is blessed.

27 Flee from evil, and do the thing that is good; * and dwell for evermore.

28 For the Lord loveth the thing that is right; * He forsaketh not His that be godly, but they are preserved for ever.

29 The unrighteous shall be punished; * as for the seed of the ungodly, it shall be rooted out.

30 The righteous shall inherit the land, * and dwell therein for ever.
31 The mouth of the righteous is exercised in wisdom, * and his tongue will be talking of judgment.
32 The law of his God is in his heart, * and his goings shall not slide.
33 The ungodly watcheth the righteous, * and seeketh occasion to slay him.
34 The Lord will not leave him in his hand, * nor condemn him when he is judged.
35 Hope thou in the Lord, and keep His way, and He shall promote thee, that thou shalt possess the land: * when the ungodly shall perish, thou shalt see it.
36 I myself have seen the ungodly in great power, * and flourishing like a green bay-tree.
37 I went by, and lo, he was gone: * I sought him, but his place could no where be found.
38 Keep innocence, and take heed unto the thing that is right; * for that shall bring a man peace at the last.
39 As for the transgressors, they shall perish together; * and the end of the ungodly is, they shall be rooted out at the last.
40 But the salvation of the righteous cometh of the Lord; * Who is also their strength in the time of trouble.
41 And the Lord shall stand by them, and save them: * He shall deliver them from the ungodly, and shall save them, because they put their trust in Him.

Eighth Day

Morning Prayer

Domine, ne in furore   Psalm 38

1 Put me not to rebuke, O Lord, in Thine anger; * neither chasten me in Thy heavy displeasure:
2 For Thine arrows stick fast in me, * and Thy hand

presseth me sore.

3 There is no health in my flesh, because of Thy displeasure; * neither is there any rest in my bones, by reason of my sin.

4 For my wickednesses are gone over my head, * and are like a sore burden, too heavy for me to bear.

5 My wounds stink, and are corrupt, * through my foolishness.

6 I am brought into so great trouble and misery, * that I go mourning all the day long.

7 For my loins are filled with a sore disease, * and there is no whole part in my body.

8 I am feeble and sore smitten; * I have roared for the very disquietness of my heart.

9 Lord, Thou knowest all my desire; * and my groaning is not hid from Thee.

10 My heart panteth, my strength hath failed me, * and the light of mine eyes is gone from me.

11 My lovers and my neighbors did stand looking upon my trouble, * and my kinsmen stood afar off.

12 They also that sought after my life laid snares for me; * and they that went about to do me evil talked of wickedness, and imagined deceit all the day long.

13 As for me, I was like a deaf man, and heard not; * and as one that is dumb, who doth not open his mouth.

14 I became even as a man that heareth not, * and in whose mouth are no reproofs.

15 For in Thee, O Lord, have I put my trust; * Thou shalt answer for me, O Lord my God.

16 I have required that they, even mine enemies, should not triumph over me; * for when my foot slipt, they rejoiced greatly against me.

17 And I truly am set in the plague, * and my heaviness is ever in my sight.

18 For I will confess my wickedness, * and be sorry for my sin.

19 But mine enemies live, and are mighty; * and they that

hate me wrongfully are many in number.
20 They also that reward evil for good are against me; *
because I follow the thing that good is.
21 Forsake me not, O Lord my God; * be not Thou far from
me.

Dixi, Custodiam   Psalm 39

1 I said, "I will take heed to my ways, * that I offend not in
my tongue.
2 I will keep my mouth as it were with a bridle, * while the
ungodly is in my sight."
3 I held my tongue, and spake nothing: * I kept silence, yea,
even from good words; but it was pain and grief to me.
4 My heart was hot within me: and while I was thus musing
the fire kindled, * and at the last I spake with my tongue:
5 "Lord, let me know mine end, and the number of my days;
* that I may be certified how long I have to live.
6 Behold, Thou hast made my days as it were a span long,
and mine age is even as nothing in respect of Thee; * and
verily every man living is altogether vanity.
7 For man walketh in a vain shadow, and disquieteth
himself in vain; * he heapeth up riches, and cannot tell who
shall gather them.
8 And now, Lord, what is my hope? * truly my hope is even
in Thee.
9 Deliver me from all mine offenses; * and make me not a
rebuke unto the foolish.
10 I became dumb, and opened not my mouth; * for it was
Thy doing.
11 Take Thy plague away from me: * I am even consumed
by the means of Thy heavy hand.
12 When Thou with rebukes dost chasten man for sin, Thou
makest his beauty to consume away, like as it were a moth
fretting a garment: * every man therefore is but vanity.
13 Hear my prayer, O Lord, and with Thine ears consider
my calling; * hold not Thy peace at my tears;

14 For I am a stranger with Thee, and a sojourner, * as all my fathers were.
15 O spare me a little, that I may recover my strength, * before I go hence, and be no more seen."

Expectans expectavi   Psalm 40

1 I waited patiently for the Lord, * and He inclined unto me, and heard my calling.
2 He brought me also out of the horrible pit, out of the mire and clay, * and set my feet upon the rock, and ordered my goings.
3 And He hath put a new song in my mouth, * even a thanksgiving unto our God.
4 Many shall see it, and fear, * and shall put their trust in the Lord.
5 Blessed is the man that hath set his hope in the Lord, * and turned not unto the proud, and to such as go about with lies.
6 O Lord my God, great are the wondrous works which Thou hast done, like as be also Thy thoughts, which are to us-ward; * and yet there is no man that ordereth them unto Thee.
7 If I should declare them, and speak of them, * they should be more than I am able to express.
8 Sacrifice and offering Thou wouldest not, * but mine ears hast Thou opened.
9 Burnt-offering and sacrifice for sin hast Thou not required: * then said I, "Lo, I come;
10 In the volume of the book it is written of me, that I should fulfill Thy will, O my God: * I am content to do it; yea, Thy law is within my heart."
11 I have declared Thy righteousness in the great congregation: * lo, I will not refrain my lips, O Lord, and that Thou knowest.
12 I have not hid Thy righteousness within my heart; * my talk hath been of Thy truth, and of Thy salvation.

13 I have not kept back Thy loving mercy and truth * from the great congregation.
14 Withdraw not Thou Thy mercy from me, O Lord; * let Thy loving-kindness and Thy truth alway preserve me.
15 For innumerable troubles are come about me; my sins have taken such hold upon me, that I am not able to look up; * yea, they are more in number than the hairs of my head, and my heart hath failed me.
16 O Lord, let it be Thy pleasure to deliver me; * make haste, O Lord, to help me.
17 Let them be ashamed, and confounded together, that seek after my soul to destroy it; * let them be driven backward, and put to rebuke, that wish me evil.
18 Let them be desolate, and rewarded with shame, * that say unto me, "Fie upon thee! fie upon thee!"
19 Let all those that seek Thee, be joyful and glad in Thee; * and let such as love Thy salvation, say alway, "The Lord be praised."
20 As for me, I am poor and needy; * but the Lord careth for me.
21 Thou art my helper and redeemer; * make no long tarrying, O my God.

Evening Prayer

Beatus qui intelligit Psalm 41

1 Blessed is he that considereth the poor and needy; * the Lord shall deliver him in the time of trouble.
2 The Lord preserve him, and keep him alive, that he may be blessed upon earth; * and deliver not Thou him into the will of his enemies.
3 The Lord comfort him when he lieth sick upon his bed; * make Thou all his bed in his sickness.
4 I said, "Lord, be merciful unto me; * heal my soul, for I have sinned against Thee."
5 Mine enemies speak evil of me, * "When shall he die, and

his name perish?"
6 And if he come to see me, he speaketh vanity, * and his
heart conceiveth falsehood within himself; and when he
cometh forth, he telleth it.
7 All mine enemies whisper together against me; * even
against me do they imagine this evil.
8 "An evil disease," say they, "cleaveth fast unto him; * and
now that he lieth, he shall rise up no more."
9 Yea, even mine own familiar friend whom I trusted, * who
did also eat of my bread, hath laid great wait for me.
10 But be Thou merciful unto me, O Lord; * raise Thou me
up again, and I shall reward them.
11 By this I know Thou favorest me, * that mine enemy doth
not triumph against me.
12 And in my innocence Thou upholdest me, * and shalt set
me before Thy face for ever.
13 Blessed be the Lord God of Israel, * world without end.
Amen.

BOOK II

Quemadmodum   Psalm 42

1 Like as the hart desireth the water-brooks, * so longeth
my soul after Thee, O God.
2 My soul is athirst for God, yea, even for the living God: *
when shall I come to appear before the presence of God?
3 My tears have been my meat day and night, * while they
daily say unto me, "Where is now thy God?"
4 Now when I think thereupon, I pour out my heart by
myself; * for I went with the multitude, and brought them
forth into the house of God;
5 In the voice of praise and thanksgiving, * among such as
keep holy-day.
6 Why art thou so full of heaviness, O my soul? * and why
art thou so disquieted within me?
7 O put thy trust in God; * for I will yet thank Him, Which is

the help of my countenance, and my God.

8 My soul is vexed within me; * therefore will I remember Thee from the land of Jordan, from Hermon and the little hill.

9 One deep calleth another, because of the noise of Thy water-floods; * all Thy waves and storms are gone over me.

10 The Lord will grant His loving-kindness in the daytime; * and in the night season will I sing of Him, and make my prayer unto the God of my life.

11 I will say unto the God of my strength, "Why hast Thou forgotten me? * why go I thus heavily, while the enemy oppresseth me?"

12 My bones are smitten asunder as with a sword, * while mine enemies that trouble me cast me in the teeth;

13 Namely, while they say daily unto me, * "Where is now thy God?"

14 Why art thou so vexed, O my soul? * and why art thou so disquieted within me?

15 O put thy trust in God; * for I will yet thank Him, Which is the help of my countenance, and my God.

Judica me, Deus   Psalm 43

1 Give sentence with me, O God, and defend my cause against the ungodly people; * O deliver me from the deceitful and wicked man.

2 For Thou art the God of my strength; why hast Thou put me from Thee? * and why go I so heavily, while the enemy oppresseth me?

3 O send out Thy light and Thy truth, that they may lead me, * and bring me unto Thy holy hill, and to Thy dwelling;

4 And that I may go unto the altar of God, even unto the God of my joy and gladness; * and upon the harp will I give thanks unto Thee, O God, my God.

5 Why art thou so heavy, O my soul? * and why art thou so disquieted within me?

6 O put thy trust in God; * for I will yet give Him thanks, Which is the help of my countenance, and my God.

Ninth Day

Morning Prayer

Deus, auribus   Psalm 44

1 We have heard with our ears, O God, our fathers have told us * what Thou hast done in their time of old:
2 How Thou hast driven out the heathen with Thy hand, and planted our fathers in; * how Thou hast destroyed the nations, and made Thy people to flourish.
3 For they got not the land in possession through their own sword, * neither was it their own arm that helped them;
4 But Thy right hand, and Thine arm, and the light of Thy countenance; * because Thou hadst a favor unto them.
5 Thou art my King, O God; * send help unto Jacob.
6 Through Thee will we overthrow our enemies, * and in Thy Name will we tread them under that rise up against us.
7 For I will not trust in my bow, * it is not my sword that shall help me;
8 But it is Thou that savest us from our enemies, * and puttest them to confusion that hate us.
9 We make our boast of God all day long, * and will praise Thy Name for ever.
10 But now Thou art far off, and puttest us to confusion, * and goest not forth with our armies.
11 Thou makest us to turn our backs upon our enemies, * so that they which hate us spoil our goods.
12 Thou lettest us be eaten up like sheep, * and hast scattered us among the heathen.
13 Thou sellest Thy people for naught, * and takest no money for them.
14 Thou makest us to be rebuked of our neighbors, * to be laughed to scorn, and had in derision of them that are round about us.

15 Thou makest us to be a by-word among the nations, * and that the peoples shake their heads at us.
16 My confusion is daily before me, * and the shame of my face hath covered me;
17 For the voice of the slanderer and blasphemer, * for the enemy and avenger.
18 And though all this be come upon us, yet do we not forget Thee, * nor behave ourselves frowardly in Thy covenant.
19 Our heart is not turned back, * neither our steps gone out of Thy way;
20 No, not when Thou hast smitten us into the place of dragons, * and covered us with the shadow of death.
21 If we have forgotten the Name of our God, and holden up our hands to any strange god, * shall not God search it out? for He knoweth the very secrets of the heart.
22 For Thy sake also are we killed all the day long, * and are counted as sheep appointed to be slain.
23 Up, Lord, why sleepest Thou? * awake, and be not absent from us for ever.
24 Wherefore hidest Thou Thy face, * and forgettest our misery and trouble?
25 For our soul is brought low, even unto the dust; * our belly cleaveth unto the ground.
26 Arise, and help us, * and deliver us, for Thy mercy's sake.

Eructavit cor meum   Psalm 45

1 My heart overfloweth with a good matter; I speak the things which I have made concerning the King. * My tongue is the pen of a ready writer.
2 Thou art fairer than the children of men; * full of grace are Thy lips, because God hath blessed Thee for ever.
3 Gird Thee with Thy sword upon Thy thigh, O Thou Most Mighty, * according to Thy worship and renown.

4 Good luck have Thou with Thine honor: * ride on, because of the word of truth, of meekness, and righteousness; and Thy right hand shall teach Thee terrible things.
5 Thy arrows are very sharp in the heart of the King's enemies, * and the people shall be subdued unto Thee.
6 Thy seat, O God, endureth for ever; * the scepter of Thy Kingdom is a right scepter.
7 Thou hast loved righteousness, and hated iniquity; * wherefore God, even Thy God, hath anointed Thee with the oil of gladness above Thy fellows.
8 All Thy garments smell of myrrh, aloes, and cassia; * out of the ivory palaces, whereby they have made Thee glad.
9 Kings' daughters are among Thy honorable women; * upon Thy right hand doth stand the queen in a vesture of gold, wrought about with divers colors.
10 Hearken, O daughter, and consider; incline thine ear; * forget also thine own people, and thy father's house.
11 So shall the King have pleasure in thy beauty; * for He is thy Lord, and worship thou Him.
12 And the daughter of Tyre shall be there with a gift; * like as the rich also among the people shall make their supplication before thee.
13 The King's daughter is all glorious within; * her clothing is of wrought gold.
14 She shall be brought unto the King in raiment of needlework: * the virgins that be her fellows shall bear her company, and shall be brought unto Thee.
15 With joy and gladness shall they be brought, * and shall enter into the King's palace.
16 Instead of Thy fathers, Thou shalt have children, * whom Thou mayest make princes in all lands.
17 I will make Thy Name to be remembered from one generation to another; * therefore shall the people give thanks unto Thee, world without end.

Deus noster refugium   Psalm 46

1 God is our hope and strength, * a very present help in
trouble.
2 Therefore will we not fear, though the earth be moved, *
and though the hills be carried into the midst of the sea;
3 Though the waters thereof rage and swell, * and though
the mountains shake at the tempest of the same.
4 There is a river, the streams whereof make glad the city
of God; * the holy place of the tabernacle of the Most
Highest.
5 God is in the midst of her, therefore shall she not be
removed; * God shall help her, and that right early.
6 The nations make much ado, and the kingdoms are
moved; * but God hath showed His voice, and the earth
shall melt away.
7 The Lord of hosts is with us; * the God of Jacob is our
refuge.
8 O come hither, and behold the works of the Lord, * what
destruction He hath brought upon the earth.
9 He maketh wars to cease in all the world; * He breaketh
the bow, and snappeth the spear in sunder, and burneth the
chariots in the fire.
10 Be still then, and know that I am God: * I will be exalted
among the nations, and I will be exalted in the earth.
11 The Lord of hosts is with us; * the God of Jacob is our
refuge.

Evening Prayer

Omnes gentes, plaudite   Psalm 47

1 Clap your hands together, all ye peoples: * O sing unto
God with the voice of melody.
2 For the Lord is high, and to be feared; * He is the great
King upon all the earth.
3 He shall subdue the peoples under us, * and the nations

under our feet.

4 He shall choose out an heritage for us, * even the excellency of Jacob, whom He loved.

5 God is gone up with a merry noise, * and the Lord with the sound of the trump.

6 O sing praises, sing praises unto our God; * O sing praises, sing praises unto our King.

7 For God is the King of all the earth: * sing ye praises with understanding.

8 God reigneth over the nations; * God sitteth upon His holy seat.

9 The princes of the peoples are joined unto the people of the God of Abraham; * for God, Which is very high exalted, doth defend the earth, as it were with a shield.

Magnus Dominus   Psalm 48

1 Great is the Lord, and highly to be praised * in the city of our God, even upon His holy hill.

2 The hill of Zion is a fair place, and the joy of the whole earth; * upon the north side lieth the city of the great King: God is well known in her palaces as a sure refuge.

3 For lo, the kings of the earth * were gathered, and gone by together.

4 They marveled to see such things; * they were astonished, and suddenly cast down.

5 Fear came there upon them; and sorrow, * as upon a woman in her travail.

6 Thou dost break the ships of the sea * through the east-wind.

7 Like as we have heard, so have we seen in the city of the Lord of hosts, in the city of our God; * God upholdeth the same for ever.

8 We wait for thy loving-kindness, O God, * in the midst of Thy temple.

9 O God, according to Thy Name, so is Thy praise unto the world's end; * Thy right hand is full of righteousness.

10 Let the mount Zion rejoice, and the daughters of Judah be glad, * because of Thy judgments.
11 Walk about Zion, and go round about her; * and tell the towers thereof.
12 Mark well her bulwarks, consider her palaces, * that ye may tell them that come after.
13 For this God is our God for ever and ever: * He shall be our guide unto death.

Audite haec, omnes   Psalm 49

1 O hear ye this, all ye people; * ponder it with your ears, all ye that dwell in the world;
2 High and low, rich and poor, * one with another.
3 My mouth shall speak of wisdom, * and my heart shall muse of understanding.
4 I will incline mine ear to the parable, * and show my dark speech upon the harp.
5 Wherefore should I fear in the days of evil, * when wickedness at my heels compasseth me round about?
6 There be some that put their trust in their goods, * and boast themselves in the multitude of their riches.
7 But no man may deliver his brother, * nor give a ransom unto God for him,
8 (For it cost more to redeem their souls, * so that he must let that alone for ever;)
9 That he shall live alway, * and not see the grave.
10 For he seeth that wise men also die and perish together, * as well as the ignorant and foolish, and leave their riches for other.
11 And yet they think that their houses shall continue for ever, and that their dwelling-places shall endure from one generation to another; * and call the lands after their own names.
12 Nevertheless, man being in honor abideth not, * seeing he may be compared unto the beasts that perish;
13 This their way is very foolishness; * yet their posterity

praise their saying.

14 They lie in the grave like sheep; death is their shepherd; and the righteous shall have dominion over them in the morning: * their beauty shall consume in the sepulcher, and have no abiding.

15 But God hath delivered my soul from the power of the grave; * for He shall receive me.

16 Be not thou afraid, though one be made rich, * or if the glory of his house be increased;

17 For he shall carry nothing away with him when he dieth, * neither shall his pomp follow him.

18 For while he lived, he counted himself an happy man; * and so long as thou doest well unto thyself, men will speak good of thee.

19 He shall follow the generation of his fathers, * and shall never see light.

20 Man that is in honor but hath no understanding * is compared unto the beasts that perish.

Tenth Day

Morning Prayer

Deus deorum   Psalm 50

1 The Lord, even the Most Mighty God, hath spoken, * and called the world, from the rising up of the sun unto the going down thereof.

2 Out of Zion hath God appeared * in perfect beauty.

3 Our God shall come, and shall not keep silence; * there shall go before Him a consuming fire, and a mighty tempest shall be stirred up round about Him.

4 He shall call the heaven from above, * and the earth, that He may judge His people.

5 "Gather My saints together unto Me; * those that have made a covenant with Me with sacrifice."

6 And the heavens shall declare His righteousness; * for God is Judge Himself.

7 "Hear, O My people, and I will speak; * I Myself will testify against thee, O Israel; for I am God, even thy God.
8 I will not reprove thee because of thy sacrifices; * as for thy burnt-offerings, they are alway before Me.
9 I will take no bullock out of thine house, * nor he-goats out of thy folds.
10 For all the beasts of the forest are Mine, * and so are the cattle upon a thousand hills.
11 I know all the fowls upon the mountains, * and the wild beasts of the field are in My sight.
12 If I be hungry, I will not tell thee; * for the whole world is Mine, and all that is therein.
13 Thinkest thou that I will eat bulls' flesh, * and drink the blood of goats?
14 Offer unto God thanksgiving, * and pay thy vows unto the Most Highest.
15 And call upon Me in the time of trouble; * so will I hear thee, and thou shalt praise Me."
16 But unto the ungodly saith God, * "Why dost thou preach My laws, and takest My covenant in thy mouth;
17 Whereas thou hatest to be reformed, * and hast cast My words behind thee?
18 When thou sawest a thief, thou consentedst unto him; * and hast been partaker with the adulterers.
19 Thou hast let thy mouth speak wickedness, * and with thy tongue thou hast set forth deceit.
20 Thou sattest and spakest against thy brother; * yea, and hast slandered thine own mother's son.
21 These things hast thou done, and I held My tongue, and thou thoughtest wickedly, that I am even such a one as thyself; * but I will reprove thee, and set before thee the things that thou hast done.
22 O consider this, ye that forget God, * lest I pluck you away, and there be none to deliver you.
23 Whoso offereth Me thanks and praise, he honoreth Me; * and to him that ordereth his way aright, will I show the salvation of God."

1 Have mercy upon me, O God, after Thy great goodness; *
according to the multitude of Thy mercies do away mine
offenses.
2 Wash me throughly from my wickedness, * and cleanse
me from my sin.
3 For I acknowledge my faults, * and my sin is ever before
me.
4 Against Thee only have I sinned, and done this evil in Thy
sight; * that Thou mightest be justified in Thy saying, and
clear when Thou shalt judge.
5 Behold, I was shapen in wickedness, * and in sin hath my
mother conceived me.
6 But lo, Thou requirest truth in the inward parts, * and shalt
make me to understand wisdom secretly.
7 Thou shalt purge me with hyssop, and I shall be clean; *
Thou shalt wash me, and I shall be whiter than snow.
8 Thou shalt make me hear of joy and gladness, * that the
bones which Thou hast broken may rejoice.
9 Turn Thy face from my sins, * and put out all my
misdeeds.
10 Make me a clean heart, O God, * and renew a right spirit
within me.
11 Cast me not away from Thy presence, * and take not
Thy Holy Spirit from me.
12 O give me the comfort of Thy help again, * and establish
me with Thy free Spirit.
13 Then shall I teach Thy ways unto the wicked, * and
sinners shall be converted unto Thee.
14 Deliver me from blood-guiltiness, O God, Thou that art
the God of my health; * and my tongue shall sing of Thy
righteousness.
15 Thou shalt open my lips, O Lord, * and my mouth shall
show Thy praise.
16 For Thou desirest no sacrifice, else would I give it Thee;

* but Thou delightest not in burnt-offerings.
17 The sacrifice of God is a troubled spirit: * a broken and contrite heart, O God, shalt Thou not despise.
18 O be favorable and gracious unto Zion; * build Thou the walls of Jerusalem.
19 Then shalt Thou be pleased with the sacrifice of righteousness, with the burnt-offerings and oblations; * then shall they offer young bullocks upon Thine altar.

Quid gloriaris?   Psalm 52

1 Why boastest thyself, thou tyrant, * that thou canst do mischief;
2 Whereas the goodness of God * endureth yet daily?
3 Thy tongue imagineth wickedness, * and with lies thou cuttest like a sharp razor.
4 Thou hast loved unrighteousness more than goodness, * and falsehood more than righteousness.
5 Thou hast loved to speak all words that may do hurt, * O thou false tongue.
6 Therefore shall God destroy thee for ever; * He shall take thee, and pluck thee out of thy dwelling, and root thee out of the land of the living.
7 The righteous also shall see this, and fear, * and shall laugh him to scorn:
8 "Lo, this is the man that took not God for his strength; * but trusted unto the multitude of his riches, and strengthened himself in his wickedness."
9 As for me, I am like a green olive-tree in the house of God; * my trust is in the tender mercy of God for ever and ever.
10 I will alway give thanks unto Thee for that Thou hast done; * and I will hope in Thy Name, for Thy saints like it well.

Evening Prayer

Dixit insipiens   Psalm 53

1 The foolish body hath said in his heart, * "There is no God."
2 Corrupt are they, and become abominable in their wickedness; * there is none that doeth good.
3 God looked down from heaven upon the children of men, * to see if there were any that would understand, and seek after God.
4 But they are all gone out of the way, they are altogether become abominable; * there is also none that doeth good, no not one.
5 Are not they without understanding that work wickedness, * eating up my people as if they would eat bread? they have not called upon God.
6 They were afraid where no fear was; * for God hath broken the bones of him that besieged thee; thou hast put them to confusion, because God hath despised them.
7 O that the salvation were given unto Israel out of Zion! * O that the Lord would deliver His people out of captivity!
8 Then should Jacob rejoice, * and Israel should be right glad.

Deus, in Nomine   Psalm 54

1 Save me, O God, for Thy Name's sake, * and avenge me in Thy strength.
2 Hear my prayer, O God, * and hearken unto the words of my mouth.
3 For strangers are risen up against me; * and tyrants, which have not God before their eyes, seek after my soul.
4 Behold, God is my helper; * the Lord is with them that uphold my soul.
5 He shall reward evil unto mine enemies: * destroy Thou them in Thy truth.

6 An offering of a free heart will I give Thee, and praise Thy Name, O Lord; * because it is so comfortable.
7 For He hath delivered me out of all my trouble; * and mine eye hath seen His desire upon mine enemies.

Exaudi, Deus   Psalm 55

1 Hear my prayer, O God, * and hide not Thyself from my petition.
2 Take heed unto me, and hear me, * how I mourn in my prayer, and am vexed;
3 The enemy crieth so, and the ungodly cometh on so fast; * for they are minded to do me some mischief, so maliciously are they set against me.
4 My heart is disquieted within me, * and the fear of death is fallen upon me.
5 Fearfulness and trembling are come upon me, * and an horrible dread hath overwhelmed me.
6 And I said, "O that I had wings like a dove! * for then would I flee away, and be at rest.
7 Lo, then would I get me away far off, * and remain in the wilderness.
8 I would make haste to escape, * because of the stormy wind and tempest."
9 Destroy their tongues, O Lord, and divide them; * for I have spied unrighteousness and strife in the city.
10 Day and night they go about within the walls thereof: * mischief also and sorrow are in the midst of it.
11 Wickedness is therein; * deceit and guile go not out of her streets.
12 For it is not an open enemy that hath done me this dishonor; * for then I could have borne it;
13 Neither was it mine adversary that did magnify himself against me; * for then peradventure I would have hid myself from him;
14 But it was even thou, my companion, * my guide, and mine own familiar friend.

15 We took sweet counsel together, * and walked in the house of God as friends.

16 Let death come hastily upon them, and let them go down alive into the pit; * for wickedness is in their dwellings, and among them.

17 As for me, I will call upon God, * and the Lord shall save me.

18 In the evening, and morning, and at noon-day will I pray, and that instantly; * and He shall hear my voice.

19 It is He that hath delivered my soul in peace from the battle that was against me; * for there were many that strove with me.

20 Yea, even God, that endureth for ever, shall hear me, and bring them down; * for they will not turn, nor fear God.

21 He laid his hands upon such as be at peace with him, * and he brake his covenant.

22 The words of his mouth were softer than butter, having war in his heart; * his words were smoother than oil, and yet be they very swords.

23 O cast thy burden upon the Lord, and He shall nourish thee, * and shall not suffer the righteous to fall for ever.

24 And as for them, * Thou, O God, shalt bring them into the pit of destruction.

25 The blood-thirsty and deceitful men shall not live out half their days: * nevertheless, my trust shall be in Thee, O Lord.

Eleventh Day

Morning Prayer

Miserere mei, Deus   Psalm 56

1 Be merciful unto me, O God, for man goeth about to devour me; * he is daily fighting, and troubling me.

2 Mine enemies are daily at hand to swallow me up; * for they be many that fight against me, O Thou Most Highest.

3 Nevertheless, though I am sometime afraid, * yet put I my trust in Thee.

4 I will praise God, because of His word: * I have put my trust in God, and will not fear what flesh can do unto me.

5 They daily mistake my words; * all that they imagine is to do me evil.

6 They hold all together, and keep themselves close, * and mark my steps, when they lay wait for my soul.

7 Shall they escape for their wickedness? * Thou, O God, in Thy displeasure shalt cast them down.

8 Thou tellest my wanderings; put my tears into Thy bottle: * are not these things noted in Thy book?

9 Whensoever I call upon Thee, then shall mine enemies be put to flight: * this I know; for God is on my side.

10 In God's word will I rejoice; * in the Lord's word will I comfort me.

11 Yea, in God have I put my trust; * I will not be afraid what man can do unto me.

12 Unto Thee, O God, will I pay my vows; * unto Thee will I give thanks.

13 For Thou hast delivered my soul from death, and my feet from falling, * that I may walk before God in the light of the living.

Miserere mei, Deus   Psalm 57

1 Be merciful unto me, O God, be merciful unto me; for my soul trusteth in Thee; * and under the shadow of Thy wings shall be my refuge, until this tyranny be overpast.

2 I will call unto the Most High God, * even unto the God that shall perform the cause which I have in hand.

3 He shall send from heaven, * and save me from the reproof of him that would eat me up.

4 God shall send forth His mercy and truth: * my soul is among lions;

5 And I lie even among the children of men, that are set on fire, * whose teeth are spears and arrows, and their tongue

a sharp sword.

6 Set up Thyself, O God, above the heavens; * and Thy glory above all the earth.

7 They have laid a net for my feet, and pressed down my soul; * they have digged a pit before me, and are fallen into the midst of it themselves.

8 My heart is fixed, O God, my heart is fixed; * I will sing and give praise.

9 Awake up, my glory; awake, lute and harp: * I myself will awake right early.

10 I will give thanks unto Thee, O Lord, among the peoples; * and I will sing unto Thee among the nations.

11 For the greatness of Thy mercy reacheth unto the heavens, * and Thy truth unto the clouds.

12 Set up Thyself, O God, above the heavens; * and Thy glory above all the earth.

Si vere utique   Psalm 58

1 Are your minds set upon righteousness, O ye congregation? * and do ye judge the thing that is right, O ye sons of men?

2 Yea, ye imagine mischief in your heart upon the earth, * and your hands deal with wickedness.

3 The ungodly are froward, even from their mother's womb; * as soon as they are born, they go astray, and speak lies.

4 They are as venomous as the poison of a serpent, * even like the deaf adder, that stoppeth her ears;

5 Which refuseth to hear the voice of the charmer, * charm he never so wisely.

6 Break their teeth, O God, in their mouths; * smite the jaw-bones of the lions, O Lord.

7 Let them fall away like water that runneth apace; * when they shoot their arrows, let them be rooted out.

8 Let them consume away like a snail, and be like the untimely fruit of a woman; * and let them not see the sun.

9 Or ever your pots be made hot with thorns, * He shall take

them away with a whirlwind, the green and the burning alike.

10 The righteous shall rejoice when he seeth the vengeance; * he shall wash his footsteps in the blood of the ungodly.

11 So that a man shall say, "Verily there is a reward for the righteous; * doubtless there is a God that judgeth the earth."

Evening Prayer

Eripe me de inimicis   Psalm 59

1 Deliver me from mine enemies, O God; * defend me from them that rise up against me.

2 O deliver me from the wicked doers, * and save me from the blood-thirsty men.

3 For lo, they lie waiting for my soul; * the mighty men are gathered against me, without any offense or fault of me, O Lord.

4 They run and prepare themselves without my fault; * arise Thou therefore to help me, and behold.

5 Stand up, O Lord God of hosts, Thou God of Israel, to visit all the heathen, * and be not merciful unto them that offend of malicious wickedness.

6 They go to and fro in the evening, * they grin like a dog, and run about through the city.

7 Behold, they speak with their mouth, and swords are in their lips; * "For who doth hear?"

8 But Thou, O Lord, shalt have them in derision, * and Thou shalt laugh all the heathen to scorn.

9 My strength will I ascribe unto Thee; * for Thou art the God of my refuge.

10 God showeth me His goodness plenteously; * and God shall let me see my desire upon mine enemies.

11 Slay them not, lest my people forget it; * but scatter them abroad among the people, and put them down, O Lord our defense.

12 For the sin of their mouth, and for the words of their lips, they shall be taken in their pride: * and why? their talk is of cursing and lies.
13 Consume them in Thy wrath, consume them, that they may perish; * and know that it is God that ruleth in Jacob, and unto the ends of the world.
14 And in the evening they will return, * grin like a dog, and will go about the city.
15 They will run here and there for meat, * and grudge if they be not satisfied.
16 As for me, I will sing of Thy power, and will praise Thy mercy betimes in the morning; * for Thou hast been my defense and refuge in the day of my trouble.
17 Unto Thee, O my strength, will I sing; * for Thou, O God, art my refuge, and my merciful God.

Deus, repulisti nos   Psalm 60

1 O God, Thou hast cast us out, and scattered us abroad; * Thou hast also been displeased: O turn Thee unto us again.
2 Thou hast moved the land, and divided it: * heal the sores thereof, for it shaketh.
3 Thou hast showed Thy people heavy things; * Thou hast given us a drink of deadly wine.
4 Thou hast given a token for such as fear Thee, * that they may triumph because of the truth.
5 Therefore were Thy beloved delivered; * help me with Thy right hand, and hear me.
6 God hath spoken in His holiness, "I will rejoice, and divide Shechem, * and mete out the Valley of Succoth.
7 Gilead is Mine, and Manasseh is Mine; * Ephraim also is the strength of My head; Judah is My law-giver;
8 Moab is My wash-pot; over Edom will I cast out My shoe; * Philistia, be thou glad of Me."
9 Who will lead me into the strong city? * who will bring me into Edom?

10 Hast not Thou cast us out, O God? * wilt not Thou, O God, go out with our hosts?
11 O be Thou our help in trouble; * for vain is the help of man.
12 Through God will we do great acts; * for it is He that shall tread down our enemies.

Exaudi, Deus   Psalm 61

1 Hear my crying, O God, * give ear unto my prayer.
2 From the ends of the earth will I call upon Thee, * when my heart is in heaviness.
3 O set me up upon the rock that is higher than I; * for Thou hast been my hope, and a strong tower for me against the enemy.
4 I will dwell in Thy tabernacle for ever, * and my trust shall be under the covering of Thy wings.
5 For Thou, O Lord, hast heard my desires, * and hast given an heritage unto those that fear Thy Name.
6 Thou shalt grant the king a long life, * that his years may endure throughout all generations.
7 He shall dwell before God for ever: * O prepare Thy loving mercy and faithfulness, that they may preserve him.
8 So will I alway sing praise unto Thy Name, * that I may daily perform my vows.

The Twelfth Day

Morning Prayer

Nonne Deo?   Psalm 62

1 My soul truly waiteth still upon God; * for of Him cometh my salvation.
2 He verily is my strength and my salvation; * He is my defense, so that I shall not greatly fall.
3 How long will ye imagine mischief against every man? *

Ye shall be slain all the sort of you; yea, as a tottering wall shall ye be, and like a broken hedge.

4 Their device is only how to put him out whom God will exalt; * their delight is in lies; they give good words with their mouth, but curse with their heart.

5 Nevertheless, my soul, wait thou still upon God; * for my hope is in Him.

6 He truly is my strength and my salvation; * He is my defense, so that I shall not fall.

7 In God is my health and my glory; * the rock of my might; and in God is my trust.

8 O put your trust in Him alway, ye people; * pour out your hearts before Him, for God is our hope.

9 As for the children of men, they are but vanity; the children of men are deceitful; * upon the weights they are altogether lighter than vanity itself.

10 O trust not in wrong and robbery; give not yourselves unto vanity: * if riches increase, set not your heart upon them.

11 God spake once, and twice I have also heard the same, * that power belongeth unto God;

12 And that Thou, Lord, art merciful; * for Thou rewardest every man according to his work.

Deus, Deus meus   Psalm 63

1 O God, Thou art my God; * early will I seek Thee.

2 My soul thirsteth for Thee, my flesh also longeth after Thee, * in a barren and dry land where no water is.

3 Thus have I looked for Thee in the sanctuary, * that I might behold Thy power and glory.

4 For Thy loving-kindness is better than the life itself: * my lips shall praise Thee.

5 As long as I live will I magnify Thee in this manner, * and lift up my hands in Thy Name.

6 My soul shall be satisfied, even as it were with marrow and fatness, * when my mouth praiseth Thee with joyful lips.

7 Have I not remembered Thee in my bed, * and thought upon Thee when I was waking?

8 Because Thou hast been my helper; * therefore under the shadow of Thy wings will I rejoice.

9 My soul hangeth upon Thee; * Thy right hand hath upholden me.

10 These also that seek the hurt of my soul, * they shall go under the earth.

11 Let them fall upon the edge of the sword, * that they may be a portion for foxes.

12 But the king shall rejoice in God; all they also that swear by Him shall be commended; * for the mouth of them that speak lies shall be stopped.

Exaudi, Deus   Psalm 64

1 Hear my voice, O God, in my prayer; * preserve my life from fear of the enemy.

2 Hide me from the gathering together of the froward, * and from the insurrection of wicked doers;

3 Who have whet their tongue like a sword, * and shoot out their arrows, even bitter words;

4 That they may privily shoot at him that is perfect: * suddenly do they hit him, and fear not.

5 They encourage themselves in mischief, * and commune among themselves, how they may lay snares; and say, that "No man shall see them."

6 They imagine wickedness, and practice it; * that they keep secret among themselves, every man in the deep of his heart.

7 But God shall suddenly shoot at them with a swift arrow, * that they shall be wounded.

8 Yea, their own tongues shall make them fall; * insomuch that whoso seeth them shall laugh them to scorn.

9 And all men that see it shall say, "This hath God done"; * for they shall perceive that it is His work.

10 The righteous shall rejoice in the Lord, and put his trust in Him; * and all they that are true of heart shall be glad.

Evening Prayer

Te decet hymnus   Psalm 65

1 Thou, O God, art praised in Zion; * and unto Thee shall the vow be performed in Jerusalem.
2 Thou that hearest the prayer, * unto Thee shall all flesh come.
3 My misdeeds prevail against me: * O be Thou merciful unto our sins.
4 Blessed is the man whom Thou choosest, and receivest unto Thee: * he shall dwell in Thy court, and shall be satisfied with the pleasures of Thy house, even of Thy holy temple.
5 Thou shalt show us wonderful things in Thy righteousness, O God of our salvation; * Thou that art the hope of all the ends of the earth, and of them that remain in the broad sea.
6 Who in His strength setteth fast the mountains, * and is girded about with power.
7 Who stilleth the raging of the sea, * and the noise of His waves, and the madness of the peoples.
8 They also that dwell in the uttermost parts of the earth shall be afraid at Thy tokens, * Thou that makest the out-goings of the morning and evening to praise Thee.
9 Thou visitest the earth, and blessest it; * Thou makest it very plenteous.
10 The river of God is full of water: * Thou preparest their corn, for so Thou providest for the earth.
11 Thou waterest her furrows; Thou sendest rain into the little valleys thereof; * Thou makest it soft with the drops of rain, and blessest the increase of it.
12 Thou crownest the year with Thy goodness; * and Thy clouds drop fatness.
13 They shall drop upon the dwellings of the wilderness; * and the little hills shall rejoice on every side.

14 The folds shall be full of sheep; * the valleys also shall stand so thick with corn, that they shall laugh and sing.

Jubilate Deo   Psalm 66

1 O be joyful in God, all ye lands; * sing praises unto the honor of His Name; make His praise to be glorious.
2 Say unto God, "O how wonderful art Thou in Thy works! * through the greatness of Thy power shall Thine enemies bow down unto Thee.
3 For all the world shall worship Thee, * sing of Thee, and praise Thy Name."
4 O come hither, and behold the works of God; * how wonderful He is in His doing toward the children of men.
5 He turned the sea into dry land, * so that they went through the water on foot; there did we rejoice thereof.
6 He ruleth with His power for ever; His eyes behold the nations: * and such as will not believe shall not be able to exalt themselves.
7 O praise our God, ye peoples, * and make the voice of His praise to be heard;
8 Who holdeth our soul in life; * and suffereth not our feet to slip.
9 For Thou, O God, hast proved us; * Thou also hast tried us, like as silver is tried.
10 Thou broughtest us into the snare; * and laidest trouble upon our loins.
11 Thou sufferedst men to ride over our heads; * we went through fire and water, and Thou broughtest us out into a wealthy place.
12 I will go into Thine house with burnt-offerings, and will pay Thee my vows, * which I promised with my lips, and spake with my mouth, when I was in trouble.
13 I will offer unto Thee fat burnt-sacrifices, with the incense of rams; * I will offer bullocks and goats.
14 O come hither, and hearken, all ye that fear God; * and I will tell you what He hath done for my soul.

15 I called unto Him with my mouth, * and gave Him praises with my tongue.
16 If I incline unto wickedness with mine heart, * the Lord will not hear me.
17 But God hath heard me; * and considered the voice of my prayer.
18 Praised be God, Who hath not cast out my prayer, * nor turned His mercy from me.

Deus misereatur Psalm 67

1 God be merciful unto us, and bless us, * and show us the light of His countenance, and be merciful unto us;
2 That Thy way may be known upon earth, * Thy saving health among all nations.
3 Let the peoples praise Thee, O God; * yea, let all the peoples praise Thee.
4 O let the nations rejoice and be glad; * for Thou shalt judge the folk righteously, and govern the nations upon earth.
5 Let the peoples praise Thee, O God; * yea, let all the peoples praise Thee.
6 Then shall the earth bring forth her increase; * and God, even our own God, shall give us His blessing.
7 God shall bless us; * and all the ends of the world shall fear Him.

Thirteenth Day

Morning Prayer

Exsurgat Deus Psalm 68

1 Let God arise, and let His enemies be scattered; * let them also that hate Him flee before Him.
2 Like as the smoke vanisheth, so shalt thou drive them away; * and like as wax melteth at the fire, so let the

ungodly perish at the presence of God.

3 But let the righteous be glad, and rejoice before God; * let them also be merry and joyful.

4 O sing unto God, and sing praises unto His Name; magnify Him that rideth upon the heavens; * praise Him in His Name JAH, and rejoice before Him.

5 He is a father of the fatherless, and defendeth the cause of the widows; * even God in His holy habitation.

6 He is the God that maketh men to be of one mind in an house, and bringeth the prisoners out of captivity; * but letteth the runagates continue in scarceness.

7 O God, when Thou wentest forth before the people; * when Thou wentest through the wilderness,

8 The earth shook, and the heavens dropped at the presence of God; * even as Sinai also was moved at the presence of God, Who is the God of Israel.

9 Thou, O God, sentest a gracious rain upon Thine inheritance, * and refreshedst it when it was weary.

10 Thy congregation shall dwell therein; * for Thou, O God, hast of Thy goodness prepared for the poor.

11 The Lord gave the word; * great was the company of women that bare the tidings.

12 "Kings with their armies did flee, and were discomfited, * and they of the household divided the spoil.

13 Though ye have lain among the sheep-folds, yet shall ye be as the wings of a dove * that is covered with silver wings, and her feathers like gold."

14 When the Almighty scattered kings for their sake, * then were they as white as snow in Salmon.

15 As the hill of Bashan, so is God's hill; * even an high hill, as the hill of Bashan.

16 Why mock ye so, ye high hills? this is God's hill, in the which it pleaseth Him to dwell; * yea, the Lord will abide in it for ever.

17 The chariots of God are twenty thousand, even thousands of angels; * and the Lord is among them as in the Holy Place of Sinai.

18 Thou art gone up on high, thou hast led captivity captive, and received gifts from men; * yea, even from thine enemies, that the Lord God might dwell among them.
19 Praised be the Lord daily, * even the God Who helpeth us, and poureth His benefits upon us.
20 He is our God, even the God of Whom cometh salvation: * God is the Lord, by Whom we escape death.
21 God shall wound the head of His enemies, * and the hairy scalp of such a one as goeth on still in his wickedness.
22 The Lord hath said, "I will bring My people again, as I did from Bashan; * Mine own will I bring again, as I did sometime from the deep of the sea.
23 That thy foot may be dipped in the blood of thine enemies, * and that the tongue of thy dogs may be red through the same."
24 It is well seen, O God, how Thou goest; * how Thou, my God and King, goest in the sanctuary.
25 The singers go before, the minstrels follow after, * in the midst of the damsels playing with the timbrels.
26 Give thanks unto God the Lord in the congregation, * ye that are of the fountain of Israel.
27 There is little Benjamin their ruler, and the princes of Judah their council; * the princes of Zebulon, and the princes of Naphthali.
28 Thy God hath sent forth strength for thee; * establish the thing, O God, that Thou hast wrought in us,
29 For Thy temple's sake at Jerusalem; * so shall kings bring presents unto Thee.
30 Rebuke Thou the dragon and the bull, with the leaders of the heathen, so that they humbly bring pieces of silver; * scatter Thou the peoples that delight in war;
31 Then shall the princes come out of Egypt; * the Morians' land shall soon stretch out her hands unto God.
32 Sing unto God, O ye kingdoms of the earth; * O sing praises unto the Lord;
33 Who sitteth in the heavens over all, from the beginning: *

lo, He doth send out His voice; yea, and that a mighty voice.

34 Ascribe ye the power to God over Israel; * His worship and strength is in the clouds.

35 O God, wonderful art Thou in Thy holy places: * even the God of Israel, He will give strength and power unto His people. Blessed be God.

Evening Prayer

Salvum me fac   Psalm 69

1 Save me, O God; * for the waters are come in, even unto my soul.

2 I stick fast in the deep mire, where no ground is; * I am come into deep waters, so that the floods run over me.

3 I am weary of crying; my throat is dry; * my sight faileth me for waiting so long upon my God.

4 They that hate me without a cause are more than the hairs of my head; * they that are mine enemies, and would destroy me guiltless, are mighty.

5 I paid them the things that I never took: * God, Thou knowest my simpleness, and my faults are not hid from Thee.

6 Let not them that trust in Thee, O Lord God of hosts, be ashamed for my cause; * let not those that seek Thee be confounded through me, O Lord God of Israel.

7 And why? for Thy sake have I suffered reproof; * shame hath covered my face.

8 I am become a stranger unto my brethren, * even an alien unto my mother's children.

9 For the zeal of Thine house hath even eaten me; * and the rebukes of them that rebuked Thee are fallen upon me.

10 I wept, and chastened myself with fasting, * and that was turned to my reproof.

11 I put on sackcloth also, * and they jested upon me.

12 They that sit in the gate speak against me, * and the

drunkards make songs upon me.

13 But, Lord, I make my prayer unto Thee * in an acceptable time.

14 Hear me, O God, in the multitude of Thy mercy, * even in the truth of Thy salvation.

15 Take me out of the mire, that I sink not; * O let me be delivered from them that hate me, and out of the deep waters.

16 Let not the water-flood drown me, neither let the deep swallow me up; * and let not the pit shut her mouth upon me.

17 Hear me, O Lord, for Thy loving-kindness is comfortable; * turn Thee unto me according to the multitude of Thy mercies.

18 And hide not Thy face from Thy servant; for I am in trouble: * O haste Thee, and hear me.

19 Draw nigh unto my soul, and save it; * O deliver me, because of mine enemies.

20 Thou hast known my reproach, my shame, and my dishonor: * mine adversaries are all in Thy sight.

21 Reproach hath broken my heart; I am full of heaviness: * I looked for some to have pity on me, but there was no man, neither found I any to comfort me.

22 They gave me gall to eat; * and when I was thirsty they gave me vinegar to drink.

23 Let their table be made a snare to take themselves withal; * and let the things that should have been for their wealth be unto them an occasion of falling.

24 Let their eyes be blinded, that they see not; * and ever bow Thou down their backs.

25 Pour out Thine indignation upon them, * and let Thy wrathful displeasure take hold of them.

26 Let their habitation be void, * and no man to dwell in their tents.

27 For they persecute him whom Thou hast smitten; * and they talk how they may vex them whom Thou hast wounded.

28 Let them fall from one wickedness to another, * and not come into Thy righteousness.
29 Let them be wiped out of the book of the living, * and not be written among the righteous.
30 As for me, when I am poor and in heaviness, * Thy help, O God, shall lift me up.
31 I will praise the Name of God with a song, * and magnify it with thanksgiving.
32 This also shall please the Lord * better than a bullock that hath horns and hoofs.
33 The humble shall consider this, and be glad: * seek ye after God, and your soul shall live.
34 For the Lord heareth the poor, * and despiseth not His prisoners.
35 Let heaven and earth praise Him: * the sea, and all that moveth therein.
36 For God will save Zion, and build the cities of Judah, * that men may dwell there, and have it in possession.
37 The posterity also of His servants shall inherit it; * and they that love His Name shall dwell therein.

Deus, in adjutorium   Psalm 70

1 Haste Thee, O God, to deliver me; * make haste to help me, O Lord.
2 Let them be ashamed and confounded that seek after my soul; * let them be turned backward and put to confusion that wish me evil.
3 Let them for their reward be soon brought to shame, * that cry over me, "There! there!"
4 But let all those that seek Thee be joyful and glad in Thee: * and let all such as delight in Thy salvation say alway, "The Lord be praised."
5 As for me, I am poor and in misery: * haste Thee unto me, O God.
6 Thou art my helper, and my redeemer: * O Lord, make no long tarrying.

Fourteenth Day

Morning Prayer

In te, Domine, speravi   Psalm 71

1 In Thee, O Lord, have I put my trust; let me never be put to confusion, * but rid me and deliver me in Thy righteousness; incline Thine ear unto me, and save me.
2 Be Thou my stronghold, whereunto I may alway resort: * Thou hast promised to help me, for Thou art my house of defense, and my castle.
3 Deliver me, O my God, out of the hand of the ungodly, * out of the hand of the unrighteous and cruel man.
4 For Thou, O Lord God, art the thing that I long for: * Thou art my hope, even from my youth.
5 Through Thee have I been holden up ever since I was born: * Thou art He that took me out of my mother's womb: my praise shall be alway of Thee.
6 I am become as it were a monster unto many, * but my sure trust is in Thee.
7 O let my mouth be filled with Thy praise, * that I may sing of Thy glory and honor all the day long.
8 Cast me not away in the time of age; * forsake me not when my strength faileth me.
9 For mine enemies speak against me; * and they that lay wait for my soul take their counsel together, saying,
10 "God hath forsaken him; * persecute him, and take him, for there is none to deliver him."
11 Go not far from me, O God; * my God, haste Thee to help me.
12 Let them be confounded and perish that are against my soul; * let them be covered with shame and dishonor that seek to do me evil.
13 As for me, I will patiently abide alway, * and will praise Thee more and more.

14 My mouth shall daily speak of Thy righteousness and salvation; * for I know no end thereof.

15 I will go forth in the strength of the Lord God, * and will make mention of Thy righteousness only.

16 Thou, O God, hast taught me from my youth up until now; * therefore will I tell of Thy wondrous works.

17 Forsake me not, O God, in mine old age, when I am gray-headed, * until I have showed Thy strength unto this generation, and Thy power to all them that are yet for to come.

18 Thy righteousness, O God, is very high, * and great things are they that Thou hast done: O God, who is like unto Thee?

19 O what great troubles and adversities hast Thou showed me! and yet didst Thou turn and refresh me; * yea, and broughtest me from the deep of the earth again.

20 Thou hast brought me to great honor, * and comforted me on every side:

21 Therefore will I praise Thee, and Thy faithfulness, O God, playing upon an instrument of music: * unto Thee will I sing upon the harp, O Thou Holy One of Israel.

22 My lips will be glad when I sing unto Thee; * and so will my soul whom Thou hast delivered.

23 My tongue also shall talk of Thy righteousness all the day long; * for they are confounded and brought unto shame that seek to do me evil.

Deus, judicium   Psalm 72

1 Give the king Thy judgments, O God, * and Thy righteousness unto the king's Son.

2 Then shall He judge Thy people according unto right, * and defend the poor.

3 The mountains also shall bring peace, * and the little hills righteousness unto the people.

4 He shall keep the simple folk by their right, * defend the children of the poor, and punish the wrong doer.

5 They shall fear Thee, as long as the sun and moon endureth, * from one generation to another.
6 He shall come down like the rain upon the mown grass, * even as the drops that water the earth.
7 In His time shall the righteous flourish; * yea, and abundance of peace, so long as the moon endureth.
8 His dominion shall be also from the one sea to the other, * and from the River unto the world's end.
9 They that dwell in the wilderness shall kneel before Him; * His enemies shall lick the dust.
10 The kings of Tarshish and of the isles shall give presents; * the kings of Arabia and Saba shall bring gifts.
11 All kings shall fall down before Him; * all nations shall do Him service.
12 For He shall deliver the poor when He crieth; * the needy also, and Him that hath no helper.
13 He shall be favorable to the simple and needy, * and shall preserve the souls of the poor.
14 He shall deliver their souls from falsehood and wrong; * and dear shall their blood be in His sight.
15 He shall live, and unto Him shall be given of the gold of Arabia; * prayer shall be made ever unto Him, and daily shall He be praised.
16 There shall be an heap of corn in the earth, high upon the hills; the fruit thereof shall shake like Lebanon: * and they of the city shall flourish like grass upon the earth.
17 His Name shall endure for ever; His Name shall remain under the sun among the posterities, which shall be blessed in Him; * and all the nations shall praise Him.
18 Blessed be the Lord God, even the God of Israel, * Which only doeth wondrous things;
19 And blessed be the Name of His majesty for ever: * and all the earth shall be filled with His majesty. Amen, Amen.

BOOK III

Evening Prayer

Quam bonus Israel!   Psalm 73

1 Truly God is loving unto Israel: * even unto such as are of a clean heart.
2 Nevertheless, my feet were almost gone, * my treadings had well-nigh slipt.
3 And why? I was grieved at the wicked: * I do also see the ungodly in such prosperity.
4 For they are in no peril of death; * but are lusty and strong.
5 They come in no misfortune like other folk; * neither are they plagued like other men.
6 And this is the cause: that they are so holden with pride, * and cruelty covereth them as a garment.
7 Their eyes swell with fatness, * and they do even what they lust.
8 They corrupt other, and speak of wicked blasphemy; * their talking is against the Most High.
9 For they stretch forth their mouth unto the heaven, * and their tongue goeth through the world.
10 Therefore fall the people unto them, * and thereout suck they no small advantage.
11 "Tush," say they, "how should God perceive it? * is there knowledge in the Most High?"
12 Lo, these are the ungodly, * these prosper in the world, and these have riches in possession:
13 And I said, "Then have I cleansed my heart in vain, * and washed my hands in innocence.
14 All the day long have I been punished, * and chastened every morning."
15 Yea, and I had almost said even as they; * but lo, then I should have condemned the generation of Thy children.
16 Then thought I to understand this; * but it was too hard

for me,
17 Until I went into the sanctuary of God: * then understood
I the end of these men;
18 Namely, how Thou dost set them in slippery places, *
and castest them down, and destroyest them.
19 O how suddenly do they consume, * perish, and come to
a fearful end!
20 Yea, even like as a dream when one awaketh; * so shalt
Thou make their image to vanish out of the city.
21 Thus my heart was grieved, * and it went even through
my reins.
22 So foolish was I, and ignorant, * even as it were a beast
before Thee.
23 Nevertheless, I am alway by Thee; * for Thou hast
holden me by my right hand.
24 Thou shalt guide me with Thy counsel, * and after that
receive me with glory.
25 Whom have I in heaven but Thee? * and there is none
upon earth that I desire in comparison of Thee.
26 My flesh and my heart faileth; * but God is the strength
of my heart, and my portion for ever.
27 For lo, they that forsake Thee shall perish; * Thou hast
destroyed all them that are unfaithful unto Thee.
28 But it is good for me to hold me fast by God, to put my
trust in the Lord God, * and to speak of all Thy works in the
gates of the daughter of Zion.

Ut quid, Deus?   Psalm 74

1 O God, wherefore art Thou absent from us so long? * why
is Thy wrath so hot against the sheep of Thy pasture?
2 O think upon Thy congregation, * whom Thou hast
purchased, and redeemed of old.
3 Think upon the tribe of Thine inheritance, * and Mount
Zion, wherein Thou hast dwelt.
4 Lift up Thy feet, that Thou mayest utterly destroy every
enemy, * which hath done evil in Thy sanctuary.

117

5 Thine adversaries roar in the midst of Thy congregations, * and set up their banners for tokens.

6 He that hewed timber afore out of the thick trees, * was known to bring it to an excellent work.

7 But now they break down all the carved work thereof * with axes and hammers.

8 They have set fire upon Thy holy places, * and have defiled the dwelling-place of Thy Name, even unto the ground.

9 Yea, they said in their hearts, "Let us make havoc of them altogether": * thus have they burnt up all the houses of God in the land.

10 We see not our tokens; there is not one prophet more; * no, not one is there among us, that understandeth any more.

11 O God, how long shall the adversary do this dishonor? * shall the enemy blaspheme Thy Name for ever?

12 Why withdrawest Thou Thy hand? * why pluckest Thou not Thy right hand out of Thy bosom to consume the enemy?

13 For God is my King of old; * the help that is done upon earth, He doeth it Himself.

14 Thou didst divide the sea through Thy power; * Thou brakest the heads of the dragons in the waters.

15 Thou smotest the heads of Leviathan in pieces, * and gavest him to be meat for the people of the wilderness.

16 Thou broughtest out fountains and waters out of the hard rocks; * Thou driedst up mighty waters.

17 The day is Thine, and the night is Thine; * Thou hast prepared the light and the sun.

18 Thou hast set all the borders of the earth; * Thou hast made summer and winter.

19 Remember this, O Lord, how the enemy hath rebuked; * and how the foolish people hath blasphemed Thy Name.

20 O deliver not the soul of Thy turtle-dove unto the multitude of the enemies; * and forget not the congregation of the poor for ever.

21 Look upon the covenant; * for all the earth is full of darkness and cruel habitations.
22 O let not the simple go away ashamed; * but let the poor and needy give praise unto Thy Name.
23 Arise, O God, maintain Thine own cause; * remember how the foolish man blasphemeth Thee daily.
24 Forget not the voice of Thine enemies: * the presumption of them that hate Thee increaseth ever more and more.

Fifteenth Day

Morning Prayer

Confitebimur tibi   Psalm 75

1 Unto Thee, O God, do we give thanks; * yea, unto Thee do we give thanks.
2 Thy Name also is so nigh; * and that do Thy wondrous works declare.
3 "In the appointed time," saith God, * "I shall judge according unto right.
4 The earth is weak, and all the inhabiters thereof: * I bear up the pillars of it."
5 I said unto the fools, "Deal not so madly"; * and to the ungodly, "Set not up your horn.
6 Set not up your horn on high, * and speak not with a stiff neck."
7 For promotion cometh neither from the east, nor from the west, * nor yet from the south.
8 And why? God is the Judge; * He putteth down one, and setteth up another.
9 For in the hand of the Lord there is a cup, and the wine is red; * it is full mixt, and He poureth out of the same.
10 As for the dregs thereof, * all the ungodly of the earth shall drink them, and suck them out.
11 But I will talk of the God of Jacob, * and praise Him for

ever.

12 All the horns of the ungodly also will I break, * and the horns of the righteous shall be exalted.

Notus in Judaea   Psalm 76

1 In Judah is God known; * His Name is great in Israel.
2 At Salem is His tabernacle, * and His dwelling in Zion.
3 There brake He the arrows of the bow, * the shield, the sword, and the battle.
4 Thou art glorious in might, * when Thou comest from the hills of the robbers.
5 The proud are robbed, they have slept their sleep; * and all the men whose hands were mighty have found nothing.
6 At Thy rebuke, O God of Jacob, * both the chariot and horse are fallen.
7 Thou, even Thou art to be feared; * and who may stand in Thy sight when Thou art angry?
8 Thou didst cause Thy judgment to be heard from heaven; * the earth trembled, and was still,
9 When God arose to judgment, * and to help all the meek upon earth.
10 The fierceness of man shall turn to Thy praise; * and the fierceness of them shalt Thou refrain.
11 Promise unto the Lord your God, and keep it, all ye that are round about Him; * bring presents unto Him that ought to be feared.
12 He shall refrain the spirit of princes, * and is wonderful among the kings of the earth.

Voce mea ad Dominum   Psalm 77

1 I Will cry unto God with my voice; * even unto God will I cry with my voice, and He shall hearken unto me.
2 In the time of my trouble I sought the Lord: * I stretched forth my hands unto Him, and ceased not in the night season; my soul refused comfort.

120

3 When I am in heaviness, I will think upon God; * when my heart is vexed, I will complain.
4 Thou holdest mine eyes waking: * I am so feeble that I cannot speak.
5 I have considered the days of old, * and the years that are past.
6 I call to remembrance my song, * and in the night I commune with mine own heart, and search out my spirit.
7 Will the Lord absent Himself for ever? * and will He be no more entreated?
8 Is His mercy clean gone for ever? * and is His promise come utterly to an end for evermore?
9 Hath God forgotten to be gracious? * and will He shut up His loving-kindness in displeasure?
10 And I said, "It is mine own infirmity; * but I will remember the years of the right hand of the Most Highest."
11 I will remember the works of the Lord, * and call to mind Thy wonders of old time.
12 I will think also of all Thy works, * and my talking shall be of Thy doings.
13 Thy way, O God, is holy: * who is so great a God as our God?
14 Thou art the God that doest wonders, * and hast declared Thy power among the peoples.
15 Thou hast mightily delivered Thy people, * even the sons of Jacob and Joseph.
16 The waters saw Thee, O God, the waters saw Thee, and were afraid; * the depths also were troubled.
17 The clouds poured out water, the air thundered, * and Thine arrows went abroad.
18 The voice of Thy thunder was heard round about: * the lightnings shone upon the ground; the earth was moved, and shook withal.
19 Thy way is in the sea, and Thy paths in the great waters, * and Thy footsteps are not known.
20 Thou leddest Thy people like sheep, * by the hand of Moses and Aaron.

Evening Prayer

Attendite, popule   Psalm 78

1 Hear my law, O my people; * incline your ears unto the words of my mouth.
2 I will open my mouth in a parable; * I will declare hard sentences of old;
3 Which we have heard and known, * and such as our fathers have told us;
4 That we should not hide them from the children of the generations to come; * but to show the honor of the Lord, His mighty and wonderful works that He hath done.
5 He made a covenant with Jacob, and gave Israel a law, * which He commanded our forefathers to teach their children;
6 That their posterity might know it, * and the children which were yet unborn;
7 To the intent that when they came up, * they might show their children the same;
8 That they might put their trust in God; * and not to forget the works of God, but to keep His commandments;
9 And not to be as their forefathers, a faithless and stubborn generation; * a generation that set not their heart aright, and whose spirit clave not steadfastly unto God;
10 Like as the children of Ephraim; * who being harnessed, and carrying bows, turned themselves back in the day of battle.
11 They kept not the covenant of God, * and would not walk in His law;
12 But forgot what He had done, * and the wonderful works that He had showed for them.
13 Marvelous things did He in the sight of our forefathers, in the land of Egypt, * even in the field of Zoan.
14 He divided the sea, and let them go through; * He made the waters to stand on an heap.

15 In the day-time also He led them with a cloud, * and all the night through with a light of fire.
16 He clave the hard rocks in the wilderness, * and gave them drink thereof, as it had been out of the great depth.
17 He brought waters out of the stony rock, * so that it gushed out like the rivers.
18 Yet for all this they sinned more against Him, * and provoked the Most Highest in the wilderness.
19 They tempted God in their hearts, * and required meat for their lust.
20 They spake against God also, saying, * "Shall God prepare a table in the wilderness?
21 He smote the stony rock indeed, that the water gushed out, and the streams flowed withal; * but can He give bread also, or provide flesh for His people?"
22 When the Lord heard this, He was wroth; * so the fire was kindled in Jacob, and there came up heavy displeasure against Israel;
23 Because they believed not in God, * and put not their trust in His help.
24 So He commanded the clouds above, * and opened the doors of heaven.
25 He rained down manna also upon them for to eat, * and gave them food from heaven.
26 So man did eat angels' food; * for He sent them meat enough.
27 He caused the east-wind to blow under heaven; * and through His power He brought in the southwest-wind.
28 He rained flesh upon them as thick as dust, * and feathered fowls like as the sand of the sea.
29 He let it fall among their tents, * even round about their habitation.
30 So they did eat, and were well filled; for He gave them their own desire: * they were not disappointed of their lust.
31 But while the meat was yet in their mouths, the heavy wrath of God came upon them, and slew the wealthiest of them; * yea, and smote down the chosen men that were in

Israel.

32 But for all this they sinned yet more, * and believed not
His wondrous works.

33 Therefore their days did He consume in vanity, * and
their years in trouble.

34 When He slew them, they sought Him, * and turned
them early, and inquired after God.

35 And they remembered that God was their strength, * and
that the High God was their Redeemer.

36 Nevertheless, they did but flatter Him with their mouth, *
and dissembled with Him in their tongue.

37 For their heart was not whole with Him, * neither
continued they steadfast in His covenant.

38 But He was so merciful, that He forgave their misdeeds,
* and destroyed them not.

39 Yea, many a time turned He His wrath away, * and
would not suffer His whole displeasure to arise.

40 For He considered that they were but flesh, * and that
they were even a wind that passeth away, and cometh not
again.

41 Many a time did they provoke Him in the wilderness, *
and grieved Him in the desert.

42 They turned back, and tempted God, * and provoked the
Holy One in Israel.

43 They thought not of His hand, * and of the day when He
delivered them from the hand of the enemy;

44 How He had wrought His miracles in Egypt, * and His
wonders in the field of Zoan.

45 He turned their waters into blood, * so that they might
not drink of the rivers.

46 He sent flies among them, and devoured them up; * and
frogs to destroy them.

47 He gave their fruit unto the caterpillar, * and their labor
unto the grasshopper.

48 He destroyed their vines with hailstones, * and their
mulberry-trees with the frost.

49 He smote their cattle also with hailstones, * and their

flocks with hot thunderbolts.

50 He cast upon them the furiousness of His wrath, anger, displeasure, and trouble: * and sent evil angels among them.

51 He made a way to His indignation, and spared not their soul from death; * but gave their life over to the pestilence;

52 And smote all the firstborn in Egypt, * the most principal and mightiest in the dwellings of Ham.

53 But as for His own people, He led them forth like sheep, * and carried them in the wilderness like a flock.

54 He brought them out safely, that they should not fear, * and overwhelmed their enemies with the sea.

55 And brought them within the borders of His sanctuary, * even to this mountain, which He purchased with His right hand.

56 He cast out the heathen also before them, * caused their land to be divided among them for an heritage, and made the tribes of Israel to dwell in their tents.

57 Yet they tempted and displeased the Most High God, * and kept not His testimonies.

58 They turned their backs, and fell away like their forefathers; * starting aside like a broken bow.

59 For they grieved Him with their hill-altars, * and provoked Him to displeasure with their images.

60 When God heard this, He was wroth, * and took sore displeasure at Israel;

61 So that He forsook the tabernacle in Shiloh, * even the tent that He had pitched among men.

62 He delivered their power into captivity, * and their beauty into the enemy's hand.

63 He gave His people over also unto the sword, * and was wroth with His inheritance.

64 The fire consumed their young men, * and their maidens were not given in marriage.

65 Their priests were slain with the sword, * and there were no widows to make lamentation.

66 So the Lord awakened as one out of sleep, * and like a

giant refreshed with wine.

67 He drove His enemies backward, * and put them to a perpetual shame.

68 He refused the tabernacle of Joseph, * and chose not the tribe of Ephraim;

69 But chose the tribe of Judah, * even the hill of Zion which He loved.

70 And there He built His temple on high, * and laid the foundation of it like the ground which He hath made continually.

71 He chose David also His servant, * and took him away from the sheep-folds:

72 As he was following the ewes with their young He took him, * that He might feed Jacob His people, and Israel His inheritance.

73 So he fed them with a faithful and true heart, * and ruled them prudently with all his power.

Sixteenth Day

Morning Prayer

Deus, venerunt   Psalm 79

1 O God, the heathen are come into Thine inheritance; * Thy holy temple have they defiled, and made Jerusalem an heap of stones.

2 The dead bodies of Thy servants have they given to be meat unto the fowls of the air, * and the flesh of Thy saints unto the beasts of the land.

3 Their blood have they shed like water on every side of Jerusalem, * and there was no man to bury them.

4 We are become an open shame to our enemies, * a very scorn and derision unto them that are round about us.

5 Lord, how long wilt Thou be angry? * shall Thy jealousy burn like fire for ever?

6 Pour out Thine indignation upon the heathen that have

not known Thee; * and upon the kingdoms that have not called upon Thy Name.

7 For they have devoured Jacob, * and laid waste His dwelling-place.

8 O remember not our old sins, but have mercy upon us, and that soon; * for we are come to great misery.

9 Help us, O God of our salvation, for the glory of Thy Name: * O deliver us, and be merciful unto our sins, for Thy Name's sake.

10 Wherefore do the heathen say, * "Where is now their God?"

11 O let the vengeance of Thy servants' blood that is shed, * be openly showed upon the heathen, in our sight.

12 O let the sorrowful sighing of the prisoners come before Thee; * according to the greatness of Thy power, preserve Thou those that are appointed to die.

13 And for the blasphemy wherewith our neighbors have blasphemed Thee, * reward Thou them, O Lord, sevenfold into their bosom.

14 So we, that are Thy people, and sheep of Thy pasture, shall give Thee thanks for ever, * and will alway be showing forth Thy praise from generation to generation.

Qui regis Israel   Psalm 80

1 Hear, O Thou Shepherd of Israel, Thou that leadest Joseph like a flock; * show Thyself also, Thou that sittest upon the Cherubim.

2 Before Ephraim, Benjamin, and Manasseh, * stir up Thy strength, and come and help us.

3 Turn us again, O God; * show the light of Thy countenance, and we shall be whole.

4 O Lord God of hosts, * how long wilt Thou be angry with Thy people that prayeth?

5 Thou feedest them with the bread of tears, * and givest them plenteousness of tears to drink.

6 Thou hast made us a very strife unto our neighbors, * and

our enemies laugh us to scorn.

7 Turn us again, Thou God of hosts; * show the light of Thy countenance, and we shall be whole.

8 Thou hast brought a vine out of Egypt; * Thou hast cast out the heathen, and planted it.

9 Thou madest room for it; * and when it had taken root, it filled the land.

10 The hills were covered with the shadow of it, * and the boughs thereof were like the goodly cedar-trees.

11 She stretched out her branches unto the sea, * and her boughs unto the River.

12 Why hast Thou then broken down her hedge, * that all they that go by pluck off her grapes?

13 The wild boar out of the wood doth root it up, * and the wild beasts of the field devour it.

14 Turn Thee again, Thou God of hosts, look down from heaven, * behold, and visit this vine;

15 And the place of the vineyard that Thy right hand hath planted, * and the branch that Thou madest so strong for Thyself.

16 It is burnt with fire, and cut down; * and they shall perish at the rebuke of Thy countenance.

17 Let Thy hand be upon the man of Thy right hand, * and upon the son of man, whom Thou madest so strong for Thine own self.

18 And so will not we go back from Thee: * O let us live, and we shall call upon Thy Name.

19 Turn us again, O Lord God of hosts; * show the light of Thy countenance, and we shall be whole.

Exultate Deo   Psalm 81

1 Sing we merrily unto God our strength; * make a cheerful noise unto the God of Jacob.

2 Take the psalm, bring hither the tabret, * the merry harp with the lute.

3 Blow up the trumpet in the New Moon, * even in the time

appointed, and upon our solemn feast-day.

4 For this was made a statute for Israel, * and a law of the God of Jacob.

5 This He ordained in Joseph for a testimony, * when He came out of the land of Egypt, and had heard a strange language.

6 I eased his shoulder from the burden, * and his hands were delivered from making the pots.

7 Thou calledst upon Me in troubles, and I delivered thee; * and heard thee what time as the storm fell upon thee.

8 I proved thee also * at the waters of strife.

9 Hear, O My people; and I will assure thee, O Israel, * if thou wilt hearken unto Me,

10 There shall no strange god be in thee, * neither shalt thou worship any other god.

11 I am the Lord thy God, Who brought thee out of the land of Egypt: * open thy mouth wide, and I shall fill it.

12 But My people would not hear My voice; * and Israel would not obey Me;

13 So I gave them up unto their own hearts' lusts, * and let them follow their own imaginations.

14 O that My people would have hearkened unto Me! * for if Israel had walked in My ways,

15 I should soon have put down their enemies, * and turned My hand against their adversaries.

16 The haters of the Lord should have submitted themselves unto Him; * but their time should have endured for ever.

17 I would have fed them also with the finest wheatflour; * and with honey out of the stony rock would I have satisfied thee.

Evening Prayer

Deus stetit   Psalm 82

1 God standeth in the congregation of princes; * He is a Judge among gods.

2 "How long will ye give wrong judgment, * and accept the persons of the ungodly?"
3 Defend the poor and fatherless; * see that such as are in need and necessity have right.
4 Deliver the outcast and poor; * save them from the hand of the ungodly.
5 They know not, neither do they understand, but walk on still in darkness: * all the foundations of the earth are out of course.
6 I have said, "Ye are gods, * and ye are all the children of the Most Highest.
7 But ye shall die like men, * and fall like one of the princes."
8 Arise, O God, and judge Thou the earth; * for Thou shalt take all nations to Thine inheritance.

Deus, quis similis?   Psalm 83

1 Hold not Thy tongue, O God, keep not still silence: * refrain not Thyself, O God.
2 For lo, Thine enemies make a murmuring; * and they that hate Thee have lift up their head.
3 They have imagined craftily against Thy people, * and taken counsel against Thy secret ones.
4 They have said, "Come, and let us root them out, that they be no more a people, * and that the name of Israel may be no more in remembrance."
5 For they have cast their heads together with one consent, * and are confederate against Thee:
6 The tabernacles of the Edomites, and the Ishmaelites; * the Moabites, and Hagarenes;
7 Gebal, and Ammon, and Amalek; * the Philistines, with them that dwell at Tyre.
8 Assyria also is joined with them; * they have holpen the children of Lot.
9 But do Thou to them as unto the Midianites; * unto Sisera, and unto Jabin at the brook of Kishon;
10 Who perished at Endor, * and became as the dung of

the earth.
11 Make them and their princes like Oreb and Zeeb; * yea, make all their princes like as Zebah and Zalmunna;
12 Who say, "Let us take to ourselves * the houses of God in possession."
13 O my God, make them like unto the whirling dust, * and as the stubble before the wind;
14 Like as the fire that burneth up the forest, * and as the flame that consumeth the mountains;
15 Pursue them even so with Thy tempest, * and make them afraid with Thy storm.
16 Make their faces ashamed, O Lord, * that they may seek Thy Name.
17 Let them be confounded and vexed ever more and more; * let them be put to shame, and perish.
18 And they shall know that Thou, Whose Name is Jehova, * art only the Most Highest over all the earth.

Quam dilecta! Psalm 84

1 O How amiable are Thy dwellings, * Thou Lord of hosts!
2 My soul hath a desire and longing to enter into the courts of the Lord; * my heart and my flesh rejoice in the living God.
3 Yea, the sparrow hath found her an house, and the swallow a nest, where she may lay her young; * even Thy altars, O Lord of hosts, my King and my God.
4 Blessed are they that dwell in Thy house; * they will be alway praising Thee.
5 Blessed is the man whose strength is in Thee; * in whose heart are Thy ways.
6 Who going through the vale of misery use it for a well; * and the pools are filled with water.
7 They will go from strength to strength, * and unto the God of gods appeareth every one of them in Zion.
8 O Lord God of hosts, hear my prayer; * hearken, O God of Jacob.
9 Behold, O God our defender, * and look upon the face of

Thine anointed.

10 For one day in Thy courts * is better than a thousand.

11 I had rather be a door-keeper in the house of my God, * than to dwell in the tents of ungodliness.

12 For the Lord God is a light and defense; * the Lord will give grace and worship; and no good thing shall He withhold from them that live a godly life.

13 O Lord God of hosts, * blessed is the man that putteth his trust in Thee.

Benedixisti, Domine   Psalm 85

1 Lord, Thou art become gracious unto Thy land; * Thou hast turned away the captivity of Jacob.

2 Thou hast forgiven the offense of Thy people, * and covered all their sins.

3 Thou hast taken away all Thy displeasure, * and turned Thyself from Thy wrathful indignation.

4 Turn us then, O God our Savior, * and let Thine anger cease from us.

5 Wilt Thou be displeased at us for ever? * and wilt Thou stretch out Thy wrath from one generation to another?

6 Wilt Thou not turn again, and quicken us, * that Thy people may rejoice in Thee?

7 Show us Thy mercy, O Lord, * and grant us Thy salvation.

8 I will hearken what the Lord God will say; * for He shall speak peace unto His people, and to His saints, that they turn not again unto foolishness.

9 For His salvation is nigh them that fear Him; * that glory may dwell in our land.

10 Mercy and truth are met together: * righteousness and peace have kissed each other.

11 Truth shall flourish out of the earth, * and righteousness hath looked down from heaven.

12 Yea, the Lord shall show loving-kindness; * and our land shall give her increase.

13 Righteousness shall go before Him, * and shall direct His going in the way.

Seventeenth Day

Morning Prayer

Inclina, Domine   Psalm 86

1 Bow down Thine ear, O Lord, and hear me; * for I am poor, and in misery.
2 Preserve Thou my soul, for I am holy: * my God, save Thy servant that putteth his trust in Thee.
3 Be merciful unto me, O Lord; * for I will call daily upon Thee.
4 Comfort the soul of Thy servant; * for unto Thee, O Lord, do I lift up my soul.
5 For Thou, Lord, art good and gracious, * and of great mercy unto all them that call upon Thee.
6 Give ear, Lord, unto my prayer, * and ponder the voice of my humble desires.
7 In the time of my trouble I will call upon Thee; * for Thou hearest me.
8 Among the gods there is none like unto Thee, O Lord; * there is not one that can do as Thou doest.
9 All nations whom Thou hast made shall come and worship Thee, O Lord; * and shall glorify Thy Name.
10 For Thou art great, and doest wondrous things: * Thou art God alone.
11 Teach me Thy way, O Lord, and I will walk in Thy truth: * O knit my heart unto Thee, that I may fear Thy Name.
12 I will thank Thee, O Lord my God, with all my heart; * and will praise Thy Name for evermore.
13 For great is Thy mercy toward me; * and Thou hast delivered my soul from the nethermost hell.
14 O God, the proud are risen against me; * and the congregations of violent men have sought after my soul, and have not set Thee before their eyes.
15 But Thou, O Lord God, art full of compassion and mercy,

133

* long-suffering, plenteous in goodness and truth.
16 O turn Thee then unto me, and have mercy upon me; *
give Thy strength unto Thy servant, and help the son of
Thine handmaid.
17 Show some token upon me for good; that they who hate
me may see it, and be ashamed, * because Thou, Lord,
hast holpen me, and comforted me.

Fundamenta ejus   Psalm 87

1 Her foundations are upon the holy hills: * the Lord loveth
the gates of Zion more than all the dwellings of Jacob.
2 Very excellent things are spoken of thee, * thou city of
God.
3 I will make mention of Egypt and Babylon, * among them
that know Me.
4 Behold, Philistia also; and Tyre, with Ethiopia; * lo, in Zion
were they born.
5 Yea, of Zion it shall be reported, this one and that one
were born in her; * and the Most High shall stablish her.
6 The Lord shall record it, when He writeth up the peoples:
* "Lo, in Zion were they born."
7 The singers also and trumpeters shall make answer: * "All
my fresh springs are in thee."

Domine, Deus   Psalm 88

1 O Lord God of my salvation, I have cried day and night
before Thee: * O let my prayer enter into Thy presence,
incline Thine ear unto my calling;
2 For my soul is full of trouble, * and my life draweth nigh
unto the grave.
3 I am counted as one of them that go down into the pit, *
and I am even as a man that hath no strength;
4 Cast off among the dead, like unto them that are slain,
and lie in the grave, * who are out of remembrance, and are
cut away from Thy hand.

5 Thou hast laid me in the lowest pit, * in a place of darkness, and in the deep.
6 Thine indignation lieth hard upon me, * and Thou hast vexed me with all Thy storms.
7 Thou hast put away mine acquaintance far from me, * and made me to be abhorred of them.
8 I am so fast in prison * that I cannot get forth.
9 My sight faileth for very trouble; * Lord, I have called daily upon Thee, I have stretched forth my hands unto Thee.
10 Dost Thou show wonders among the dead? * or shall the dead rise up again, and praise Thee?
11 Shall Thy loving-kindness be showed in the grave? * or Thy faithfulness in destruction?
12 Shall Thy wondrous works be known in the dark? * and Thy righteousness in the land where all things are forgotten?
13 Unto Thee have I cried, O Lord; * and early shall my prayer come before Thee.
14 Lord, why abhorrest Thou my soul, * and hidest Thou Thy face from me?
15 I am in misery, and like unto him that is at the point to die; * even from my youth up, Thy terrors have I suffered with a troubled mind.
16 Thy wrathful displeasure goeth over me, * and the fear of Thee hath undone me.
17 They came round about me daily like water, * and compassed me together on every side.
18 My lovers and friends hast Thou put away from me, * and hid mine acquaintance out of my sight.

Evening Prayer

Misericordias Domini   Psalm 89

1 My song shall be alway of the loving-kindness of the Lord; * with my mouth will I ever be showing Thy truth from one generation to another.

2 For I have said, "Mercy shall be set up for ever; * Thy truth shalt Thou establish in the heavens.
3 I have made a covenant with My chosen; * I have sworn unto David My servant:
4 'Thy seed will I establish for ever, * and set up thy throne from one generation to another.'"
5 O Lord, the very heavens shall praise Thy wondrous works; * and Thy truth in the congregation of the saints.
6 For who is he among the clouds, * that shall be compared unto the Lord?
7 And what is he among the gods, * that shall be like unto the Lord?
8 God is very greatly to be feared in the council of the saints, * and to be had in reverence of all them that are round about Him.
9 O Lord God of hosts, who is like unto Thee? * Thy truth, most mighty Lord, is on every side.
10 Thou rulest the raging of the sea; * Thou stillest the waves thereof when they arise.
11 Thou hast subdued Egypt, and destroyed it; * Thou hast scattered Thine enemies abroad with Thy mighty arm.
12 The heavens are Thine, the earth also is Thine; * Thou hast laid the foundation of the round world, and all that therein is.
13 Thou hast made the north and the south; * Tabor and Hermon shall rejoice in Thy Name.
14 Thou hast a mighty arm; * strong is Thy hand, and high is Thy right hand.
15 Righteousness and equity are the habitation of Thy seat; * mercy and truth shall go before Thy face.
16 Blessed is the people, O Lord, that can rejoice in Thee; * they shall walk in the light of Thy countenance.
17 Their delight shall be daily in Thy Name; * and in Thy righteousness shall they make their boast.
18 For Thou art the glory of their strength, * and in Thy loving-kindness Thou shalt lift up our horns.

19 For the Lord is our defense; * the Holy One of Israel is our King.
20 Thou spakest sometime in visions unto Thy saints, and saidst, * "I have laid help upon one that is mighty, I have exalted one chosen out of the people.
21 I have found David My servant; * with My holy oil have I anointed him.
22 My hand shall hold him fast, * and My arm shall strengthen him.
23 The enemy shall not be able to do him violence; * the son of wickedness shall not hurt him.
24 I will smite down his foes before his face, * and plague them that hate him.
25 My truth also and My mercy shall be with him; * and in My Name shall his horn be exalted.
26 I will set his dominion also in the sea, * and his right hand in the floods.
27 He shall call me, 'Thou art my Father, * my God, and my strong salvation.'
28 And I will make him My firstborn, * higher than the kings of the earth.
29 My mercy will I keep for him for evermore, * and My covenant shall stand fast with him.
30 His seed also will I make to endure for ever, * and his throne as the days of heaven.
31 But if his children forsake My law, * and walk not in My judgments;
32 If they break My statutes, and keep not My commandments; * I will visit their offenses with the rod, and their sin with scourges.
33 Nevertheless, My loving-kindness will I not utterly take from him, * nor suffer My truth to fail.
34 My covenant will I not break, nor alter the thing that is gone out of My lips: * I have sworn once by My holiness, that I will not fail David.
35 His seed shall endure for ever, * and his throne is like as the sun before Me.

36 He shall stand fast for evermore as the moon, * and as the faithful witness in heaven."
37 But Thou hast abhorred and forsaken Thine anointed, * and art displeased at him.
38 Thou hast broken the covenant of Thy servant, * and cast his crown to the ground.
39 Thou hast overthrown all his hedges, * and broken down his strongholds.
40 All they that go by spoil him, * and he is become a reproach to his neighbors.
41 Thou hast set up the right hand of his enemies, * and made all his adversaries to rejoice.
42 Thou hast taken away the edge of his sword, * and givest him not victory in the battle.
43 Thou hast put out his glory, * and cast his throne down to the ground.
44 The days of his youth hast Thou shortened, * and covered him with dishonor.
45 Lord, how long wilt Thou hide Thyself? for ever? * and shall Thy wrath burn like fire?
46 O remember how short my time is; * wherefore hast Thou made all men for naught?
47 What man is he that liveth, and shall not see death? * and shall he deliver his soul from the power of the grave?
48 Lord, where are Thy old loving-kindnesses, * which Thou swarest unto David in Thy truth?
49 Remember, Lord, the rebuke that Thy servants have, * and how I do bear in my bosom the rebukes of many people;
50 Wherewith Thine enemies have blasphemed Thee, * and slandered the footsteps of Thine anointed.
51 Praised be the Lord for evermore. * Amen, and Amen.

BOOK IV

The Eighteenth Day

Morning Prayer

Domine, refugium   Psalm 90

1 Lord, Thou hast been our refuge, * from one generation to another.
2 Before the mountains were brought forth, or ever the earth and the world were made, * Thou art God from everlasting, and world without end.
3 Thou turnest man to destruction; * again Thou sayest, "Come again, ye children of men."
4 For a thousand years in Thy sight are but as yesterday when it is past, * and as a watch in the night.
5 As soon as Thou scatterest them they are even as a sleep; * and fade away suddenly like the grass.
6 In the morning it is green, and groweth up; * but in the evening it is cut down, dried up, and withered.
7 For we consume away in Thy displeasure, * and are afraid at Thy wrathful indignation.
8 Thou hast set our misdeeds before Thee; * and our secret sins in the light of Thy countenance.
9 For when Thou art angry all our days are gone: * we bring our years to an end, as it were a tale that is told.
10 The days of our age are threescore years and ten; and though men be so strong that they come to fourscore years, * yet is their strength then but labor and sorrow; so soon passeth it away, and we are gone.
11 But who regardeth the power of Thy wrath? * or feareth aright Thy indignation?
12 So teach us to number our days, * that we may apply our hearts unto wisdom.
13 Turn Thee again, O Lord, at the last, * and be gracious unto Thy servants.
14 O satisfy us with Thy mercy, and that soon: * so shall we

rejoice and be glad all the days of our life.

15 Comfort us again now after the time that Thou hast plagued us; * and for the years wherein we have suffered adversity.

16 Show Thy servants Thy work, * and their children Thy glory.

17 And the glorious majesty of the Lord our God be upon us: * prosper Thou the work of our hands upon us; O prosper Thou our handy-work.

Qui habitat   Psalm 91

1 Whoso dwelleth under the defense of the Most High, * shall abide under the shadow of the Almighty.

2 I will say unto the Lord, "Thou art my hope, and my stronghold; * my God, in Him will I trust."

3 For He shall deliver thee from the snare of the hunter, * and from the noisome pestilence.

4 He shall defend thee under His wings, and thou shalt be safe under His feathers; * His faithfulness and truth shall be thy shield and buckler.

5 Thou shalt not be afraid for any terror by night, * nor for the arrow that flieth by day;

6 For the pestilence that walketh in darkness, * nor for the sickness that destroyeth in the noon-day.

7 A thousand shall fall beside thee, and ten thousand at thy right hand; * but it shall not come nigh thee.

8 Yea, with thine eyes shalt thou behold, * and see the reward of the ungodly.

9 For Thou, Lord, art my hope. * Thou hast set thine house of defense very high.

10 There shall no evil happen unto thee, * neither shall any plague come nigh thy dwelling.

11 For He shall give His angels charge over thee, * to keep thee in all thy ways.

12 They shall bear thee in their hands, * that thou hurt not thy foot against a stone.

13 Thou shalt go upon the lion and adder: * the young lion

and the dragon shalt thou tread under thy feet.
14 "Because he hath set his love upon Me, therefore will I deliver him; * I will set him up, because he hath known My Name.
15 He shall call upon Me, and I will hear him; * yea, I am with him in trouble; I will deliver him, and bring him to honor.
16 With long life will I satisfy him, * and show him My salvation."

Bonum est confiteri   Psalm 92

1 It is a good thing to give thanks unto the Lord, * and to sing praises unto Thy Name, O Most Highest;
2 To tell of Thy loving-kindness early in the morning, * and of Thy truth in the night season;
3 Upon an instrument of ten strings, and upon the lute; * upon a loud instrument, and upon the harp.
4 For Thou, Lord, hast made me glad through Thy works; * and I will rejoice in giving praise for the operations of Thy hands.
5 O Lord, how glorious are Thy works! * Thy thoughts are very deep.
6 An unwise man doth not well consider this, * and a fool doth not understand it.
7 When the ungodly are green as the grass, and when all the workers of wickedness do flourish, * then shall they be destroyed for ever; but Thou, Lord, art the Most Highest for evermore.
8 For lo, Thine enemies, O Lord, lo, Thine enemies shall perish; * and all the workers of wickedness shall be destroyed.
9 But my horn shall be exalted like the horn of an unicorn; * for I am anointed with fresh oil.
10 Mine eye also shall see his lust of mine enemies, * and mine ear shall hear his desire of the wicked that arise up against me.
11 The righteous shall flourish like a palm-tree, * and shall spread abroad like a cedar in Lebanon.

12 Such as are planted in the house of the Lord, * shall flourish in the courts of the house of our God.
13 They also shall bring forth more fruit in their age, * and shall be fat and well-liking;
14 That they may show how true the Lord my strength is, * and that there is no unrighteousness in Him.

Evening Prayer

Dominus regnavit   Psalm 93

1 The Lord is King, and hath put on glorious apparel; * the Lord hath put on His apparel, and girded Himself with strength.
2 He hath made the round world so sure, * that it cannot be moved.
3 Ever since the world began, hath Thy seat been prepared: * Thou art from everlasting.
4 The floods are risen, O Lord, the floods have lift up their voice; * the floods lift up their waves.
5 The waves of the sea are mighty, and rage horribly; * but yet the Lord, Who dwelleth on high, is mightier.
6 Thy testimonies, O Lord, are very sure: * holiness becometh Thine house for ever.

Deus ultionum   Psalm 94

1 O Lord God, to Whom vengeance belongeth, * Thou God, to Whom vengeance belongeth, show Thyself.
2 Arise, Thou Judge of the world, * and reward the proud after their deserving.
3 Lord, how long shall the ungodly, * how long shall the ungodly triumph?
4 How long shall all wicked doers speak so disdainfully, * and make such proud boasting?
5 They smite down Thy people, O Lord, * and trouble Thine heritage.
6 They murder the widow and the stranger, * and put the

fatherless to death.

7 And yet they say, "Tush, the Lord shall not see, * neither shall the God of Jacob regard it."

8 Take heed, ye unwise among the people: * O ye fools, when will ye understand?

9 He that planted the ear, shall He not hear? * or He that made the eye, shall He not see?

10 Or He that instructeth the heathen, * it is He that teacheth man knowledge; shall not He punish?

11 The Lord knoweth the thoughts of man, * that they are but vain.

12 Blessed is the man whom Thou chastenest, O Lord, * and teachest him in Thy law;

13 That Thou mayest give him patience in time of adversity, * until the pit be digged up for the ungodly.

14 For the Lord will not fail His people; * neither will He forsake His inheritance;

15 Until righteousness turn again unto judgment: * all such as are true in heart shall follow it.

16 Who will rise up with me against the wicked? * or who will take my part against the evil doers?

17 If the Lord had not helped me, * it had not failed, but my soul had been put to silence.

18 But when I said, "My foot hath slipt," * Thy mercy, O Lord, held me up.

19 In the multitude of the sorrows that I had in my heart, * Thy comforts have refreshed my soul.

20 Wilt Thou have any thing to do with the throne of wickedness, * which imagineth mischief as a law?

21 They gather them together against the soul of the righteous, * and condemn the innocent blood.

22 But the Lord is my refuge, * and my God is the strength of my confidence.

23 He shall recompense them their wickedness, and destroy them in their own malice; * yea, the Lord our God shall destroy them.

Nineteenth Day

Morning Prayer

Venite, exultemus   Psalm 95

1 O come, let us sing unto the Lord; * let us heartily rejoice in the strength of our salvation.
2 Let us come before His presence with thanksgiving; * and show ourselves glad in Him with psalms.
3 For the Lord is a great God; * and a great King above all gods.
4 In His hand are all the corners of the earth; * and the strength of the hills is His also.
5 The sea is His, and He made it; * and His hands prepared the dry land.
6 O come, let us worship and fall down, * and kneel before the Lord our Maker.
7 For He is the Lord our God; * and we are the people of His pasture, and the sheep of His hand.
8 Today if ye will hear His voice: "Harden not your hearts * as in the provocation, and as in the day of temptation in the wilderness;
9 When your fathers tempted Me, * proved Me, and saw My works.
10 Forty years long was I grieved with this generation, and said, * 'It is a people that do err in their hearts, for they have not known My ways':
11 Unto whom I sware in My wrath, * that they should not enter into My rest."

Cantate Domino   Psalm 96

1 O sing unto the Lord a new song; * sing unto the Lord, all the whole earth.
2 Sing unto the Lord, and praise His Name; * be telling of His salvation from day to day.
3 Declare His honor unto the heathen, * and His wonders

unto all peoples.

4 For the Lord is great, and cannot worthily be praised;* He is more to be feared than all gods.

5 As for all the gods of the heathen, they are but idols; * but it is the Lord that made the heavens.

6 Glory and worship are before Him; * power and honor are in His sanctuary.

7 Ascribe unto the Lord, O ye kindreds of the peoples, * ascribe unto the Lord worship and power.

8 Ascribe unto the Lord the honor due unto His Name; * bring presents, and come into His courts.

9 O worship the Lord in the beauty of holiness; * let the whole earth stand in awe of Him.

10 Tell it out among the heathen, that the Lord is King, and that it is He Who hath made the round world so fast that it cannot be moved; * and how that He shall judge the peoples righteously.

11 Let the heavens rejoice, and let the earth be glad; * let the sea make a noise, and all that therein is.

12 Let the field be joyful, and all that is in it; * then shall all the trees of the wood rejoice before the Lord.

13 For He cometh, for He cometh to judge the earth; * and with righteousness to judge the world, and the peoples with His truth.

Dominus regnavit   Psalm 97

1 The Lord is King, the earth may be glad thereof; * yea, the multitude of the isles may be glad thereof.

2 Clouds and darkness are round about Him: * righteousness and judgment are the habitation of His seat.

3 There shall go a fire before Him, * and burn up His enemies on every side.

4 His lightnings gave shine unto the world: * the earth saw it, and was afraid.

5 The hills melted like wax at the presence of the Lord; * at the presence of the Lord of the whole earth.

6 The heavens have declared His righteousness, * and all

the peoples have seen His glory.

7 Confounded be all they that worship carved images, and that delight in vain gods: * worship Him, all ye gods.

8 Zion heard of it, and rejoiced; and the daughters of Judah were glad, * because of Thy judgments, O Lord.

9 For Thou, Lord, art higher than all that are in the earth: * Thou art exalted far above all gods.

10 O ye that love the Lord, see that ye hate the thing which is evil: * the Lord preserveth the souls of His saints; He shall deliver them from the hand of the ungodly.

11 There is sprung up a light for the righteous, * and joyful gladness for such as are true-hearted.

12 Rejoice in the Lord, ye righteous; * and give thanks for a remembrance of His holiness.

Evening Prayer

Cantate Domino Psalm 98

1 O sing unto the Lord a new song; * for He hath done marvelous things.

2 With His own right hand, and with His holy arm, * hath He gotten Himself the victory.

3 The Lord declared His salvation; * His righteousness hath He openly showed in the sight of the heathen.

4 He hath remembered His mercy and truth toward the house of Israel; * and all the ends of the world have seen the salvation of our God.

5 Show yourselves joyful unto the Lord, all ye lands; * sing, rejoice, and give thanks.

6 Praise the Lord upon the harp; * sing to the harp with a psalm of thanksgiving.

7 With trumpets also and shawms, * O show yourselves joyful before the Lord, the King.

8 Let the sea make a noise, and all that therein is; * the round world, and they that dwell therein.

9 Let the floods clap their hands, and let the hills be joyful together before the Lord; * for He is come to judge the

earth.

10 With righteousness shall He judge the world, * and the peoples with equity.

Dominus regnavit   Psalm 99

1 The Lord is King, be the people never so impatient; * He sitteth between the Cherubim, be the earth never so unquiet.

2 The Lord is great in Zion, * and high above all people.

3 They shall give thanks unto Thy Name, * Which is great, wonderful, and holy.

4 The King's power loveth judgment; Thou hast prepared equity, * Thou hast executed judgment and righteousness in Jacob.

5 O magnify the Lord our God, and fall down before His footstool; * for He is holy.

6 Moses and Aaron among His priests, and Samuel among such as call upon His Name: * these called upon the Lord, and He heard them.

7 He spake unto them out of the cloudy pillar; * for they kept His testimonies, and the law that He gave them.

8 Thou heardest them, O Lord our God; * Thou forgavest them, O God, though Thou didst punish their wicked doings.

9 O magnify the Lord our God, and worship Him upon His holy hill; * for the Lord our God is holy.

Jubilate Deo   Psalm 100

1 O be joyful in the Lord, all ye lands: * serve the Lord with gladness, and come before His presence with a song.

2 Be ye sure that the Lord He is God; it is He that hath made us, and not we ourselves; * we are His people, and the sheep of His pasture.

3 O go your way into His gates with thanksgiving, and into His courts with praise; * be thankful unto Him, and speak good of His Name.

147

4 For the Lord is gracious, His mercy is everlasting; * and His truth endureth from generation to generation.

Misericordiam et judicium   Psalm 101

1 My song shall be of mercy and judgment; * unto Thee, O Lord, will I sing.
2 O let me have understanding * in the way of godliness!
3 When wilt Thou come unto me? * I will walk in my house with a perfect heart.
4 I will take no wicked thing in hand; I hate the sins of unfaithfulness; * there shall no such cleave unto me.
5 A froward heart shall depart from me; * I will not know a wicked person.
6 Whoso privily slandereth his neighbor, * him will I destroy.
7 Whoso hath also a haughty look and a proud heart, * I will not suffer him.
8 Mine eyes look upon such as are faithful in the land, * that they may dwell with me.
9 Whoso leadeth a godly life, * he shall be my servant.
10 There shall no deceitful person dwell in my house; * he that telleth lies shall not tarry in my sight.
11 I shall soon destroy all the ungodly that are in the land; * that I may root out all wicked doers from the city of the Lord.

Twentieth Day

Morning Prayer

Domine, exaudi   Psalm 102

1 Hear my prayer, O Lord, * and let my crying come unto Thee.
2 Hide not Thy face from me in the time of my trouble; * incline Thine ear unto me when I call; O hear me, and that right soon.
3 For my days are consumed away like smoke, * and my bones are burnt up as it were a firebrand.

4 My heart is smitten down, and withered like grass; * so that I forget to eat my bread.

5 For the voice of my groaning, * my bones will scarce cleave to my flesh.

6 I am become like a pelican in the wilderness, * and like an owl that is in the desert.

7 I have watched, and am even as it were a sparrow, * that sitteth alone upon the housetop.

8 Mine enemies revile me all the day long; * and they that are mad upon me are sworn together against me.

9 For I have eaten ashes as it were bread, * and mingled my drink with weeping;

10 And that, because of Thine indignation and wrath; * for Thou hast taken me up, and cast me down.

11 My days are gone like a shadow, * and I am withered like grass.

12 But Thou, O Lord, shalt endure for ever, * and Thy remembrance throughout all generations.

13 Thou shalt arise, and have mercy upon Zion; * for it is time that Thou have mercy upon her, yea, the time is come.

14 And why? Thy servants think upon her stones, * and it pitieth them to see her in the dust.

15 The nations shall fear Thy Name, O Lord; * and all the kings of the earth Thy majesty;

16 When the Lord shall build up Zion, * and when His glory shall appear;

17 When He turneth Him unto the prayer of the poor destitute, * and despiseth not their desire.

18 This shall be written for those that come after, * and the people which shall be born shall praise the Lord.

19 For He hath looked down from His sanctuary; * out of the heaven did the Lord behold the earth;

20 That He might hear the mournings of such as are in captivity, * and deliver them that are appointed unto death;

21 That they may declare the Name of the Lord in Zion, * and His worship at Jerusalem;

22 When the peoples are gathered together, * and the

kingdoms also, to serve the Lord.
23 He brought down my strength in my journey, * and shortened my days.
24 But I said, "O my God, take me not away in the midst of mine age; * as for Thy years, they endure throughout all generations.
25 Thou, Lord, in the beginning hast laid the foundation of the earth, * and the heavens are the work of Thy hands.
26 They shall perish, but Thou shalt endure: * they all shall wax old as doth a garment;
27 And as a vesture shalt Thou change them, and they shall be changed; * but Thou art the same, and Thy years shall not fail.
28 The children of Thy servants shall continue, * and their seed shall stand fast in Thy sight."

Benedic, anima mea   Psalm 103

1 Praise the Lord, O my soul; * and all that is within me, praise His holy Name.
2 Praise the Lord, O my soul, * and forget not all His benefits:
3 Who forgiveth all thy sin, * and healeth all thine infirmities;
4 Who saveth thy life from destruction, * and crowneth thee with mercy and loving-kindness;
5 Who satisfieth thy mouth with good things, * making thee young and lusty as an eagle.
6 The Lord executeth righteousness and judgment * for all them that are oppressed with wrong.
7 He showed His ways unto Moses, * His works unto the children of Israel.
8 The Lord is full of compassion and mercy, * longsuffering, and of great goodness.
9 He will not alway be chiding; * neither keepeth He His anger for ever.
10 He hath not dealt with us after our sins; * nor rewarded us according to our wickednesses.

11 For look how high the heaven is in comparison of the earth; * so great is His mercy also toward them that fear Him.
12 Look how wide also the east is from the west; * so far hath He set our sins from us.
13 Yea, like as a father pitieth His own children; * even so is the Lord merciful unto them that fear Him.
14 For He knoweth whereof we are made; * He remembereth that we are but dust.
15 The days of man are but as grass; * for He flourisheth as a flower of the field.
16 For as soon as the wind goeth over it, it is gone; * and the place thereof shall know it no more.
17 But the merciful goodness of the Lord endureth for ever and ever upon them that fear Him; * and His righteousness upon children's children;
18 Even upon such as keep His covenant, * and think upon His commandments to do them.
19 The Lord hath prepared His seat in heaven, * and His kingdom ruleth over all.
20 O praise the Lord, ye angels of His, ye that excel in strength; * ye that fulfill His commandment, and hearken unto the voice of His word.
21 O praise the Lord, all ye His hosts; * ye servants of His that do His pleasure.
22 O speak good of the Lord, all ye works of His, in all places of His dominion: * praise thou the Lord, O my soul.

Evening Prayer

Benedic, anima mea   Psalm 104

1 Praise the Lord, O my soul: * O Lord my God, Thou art become exceeding glorious; Thou art clothed with majesty and honor.
2 Thou deckest Thyself with light as it were with a garment, * and spreadest out the heavens like a curtain.

3 Who layeth the beams of His chambers in the waters, * and maketh the clouds His chariot, and walketh upon the wings of the wind.

4 He maketh His angels winds, * and His ministers a flaming fire.

5 He laid the foundations of the earth, * that it never should move at any time.

6 Thou coveredst it with the deep like as with a garment; * the waters stand above the hills.

7 At Thy rebuke they flee; * at the voice of Thy thunder they haste away.

8 They go up as high as the hills, and down to the valleys beneath; * even unto the place which Thou hast appointed for them.

9 Thou hast set them their bounds, which they shall not pass, * neither turn again to cover the earth.

10 He sendeth the springs into the rivers, * which run among the hills.

11 All beasts of the field drink thereof, * and the wild asses quench their thirst.

12 Beside them shall the fowls of the air have their habitation, * and sing among the branches.

13 He watereth the hills from above; * the earth is filled with the fruit of Thy works.

14 He bringeth forth grass for the cattle, * and green herb for the service of men;

15 That he may bring food out of the earth, and wine that maketh glad the heart of man; * and oil to make him a cheerful countenance, and bread to strengthen man's heart.

16 The trees of the Lord also are full of sap; * even the cedars of Lebanon which He hath planted;

17 Wherein the birds make their nests; * and the firtrees are a dwelling for the stork.

18 The high hills are a refuge for the wild goats; * and so are the stony rocks for the conies.

19 He appointed the moon for certain seasons, * and the sun knoweth his going down.

20 Thou makest darkness that it may be night; * wherein all the beasts of the forest do move.

21 The lions, roaring after their prey, * do seek their meat from God.

22 The sun ariseth, and they get them away together, * and lay them down in their dens.

23 Man goeth forth to his work, and to his labor, * until the evening.

24 O Lord, how manifold are Thy works! * in wisdom hast Thou made them all; the earth is full of Thy riches.

25 So is the great and wide sea also; * wherein are things creeping innumerable, both small and great beasts.

26 There go the ships, and there is that Leviathan, * whom Thou hast made to take his pastime therein.

27 These wait all upon Thee, * that Thou mayest give them meat in due season.

28 When Thou givest it them, they gather it; * and when Thou openest Thy hand, they are filled with good.

29 When Thou hidest Thy face, they are troubled: * when Thou takest away their breath, they die, and are turned again to their dust.

30 When Thou lettest Thy breath go forth, they shall be made; * and Thou shalt renew the face of the earth.

31 The glorious majesty of the Lord shall endure for ever; * the Lord shall rejoice in His works.

32 The earth shall tremble at the look of Him; * if He do but touch the hills, they shall smoke.

33 I will sing unto the Lord as long as I live; * I will praise my God while I have my being.

34 And so shall my words please Him: * my joy shall be in the Lord.

35 As for sinners, they shall be consumed out of the earth, * and the ungodly shall come to an end.

36 Praise thou the Lord, O my soul. * Praise the Lord.

Morning Prayer

Confitemini Domino   Psalm 105

1 Give thanks unto the Lord, and call upon His Name; * tell the people what things He hath done.
2 O let your songs be of Him, and praise Him; * and let your talking be of all His wondrous works.
3 Rejoice in His holy Name; * let the heart of them rejoice that seek the Lord.
4 Seek the Lord and His strength; * seek His face evermore.
5 Remember the marvelous works that He hath done; * His wonders, and the judgments of His mouth;
6 O ye seed of Abraham His servant, * ye children of Jacob His chosen.
7 He is the Lord our God; * His judgments are in all the world.
8 He hath been alway mindful of His covenant and promise, * that He made to a thousand generations;
9 Even the covenant that He made with Abraham; * and the oath that He sware unto Isaac;
10 And appointed the same unto Jacob for a law, * and to Israel for an everlasting testament;
11 Saying, "Unto thee will I give the land of Canaan, * the lot of your inheritance,"
12 When there were yet but a few of them, * and they strangers in the land.
13 What time as they went from one nation to another, * from one kingdom to another people;
14 He suffered no man to do them wrong, * but reproved even kings for their sakes;
15 Touch not Mine anointed, * and do My prophets no harm.
16 Moreover, He called for a dearth upon the land, * and

destroyed all the provision of bread.

17 But He had sent a man before them, * even Joseph, who was sold to be a bond-servant;

18 Whose feet they hurt in the stocks; * the iron entered into his soul;

19 Until the time came that his cause was known: * the word of the Lord tried him.

20 The king sent, and delivered him; * the prince of the people let him go free.

21 He made him lord also of his house, * and ruler of all his substance;

22 That he might inform his princes after his will, * and teach his senators wisdom.

23 Israel also came into Egypt, * and Jacob was a stranger in the land of Ham.

24 And He increased His people exceedingly, * and made them stronger than their enemies;

25 Whose heart turned so, that they hated His people, * and dealt untruly with His servants.

26 Then sent He Moses His servant, * and Aaron whom He had chosen.

27 And these showed His tokens among them, * and wonders in the land of Ham.

28 He sent darkness, and it was dark; * and they were not obedient unto His word.

29 He turned their waters into blood, * and slew their fish.

30 Their land brought forth frogs; * yea, even in their kings' chambers.

31 He spake the word, and there came all manner of flies, * and lice in all their quarters.

32 He gave them hailstones for rain; * and flames of fire in their land.

33 He smote their vines also and fig-trees; * and destroyed the trees that were in their coasts.

34 He spake the word, and the grasshoppers came, and caterpillars innumerable, * and did eat up all the grass in their land, and devoured the fruit of their ground.

35 He smote all the firstborn in their land; * even the chief of all their strength.
36 He brought them forth also with silver and gold; * there was not one feeble person among their tribes.
37 Egypt was glad at their departing; * for they were afraid of them.
38 He spread out a cloud to be a covering, * and fire to give light in the night season.
39 At their desire He brought quails; * and He filled them with the bread of heaven.
40 He opened the rock of stone, and the waters flowed out, * so that rivers ran in the dry places.
41 For why? He remembered His holy promise; * and Abraham His servant.
42 And He brought forth His people with joy, * and His chosen with gladness;
43 And gave them the lands of the heathen; * and they took the labors of the people in possession;
44 That they might keep His statutes, * and observe His laws.

Evening Prayer

Confitemini Domino   Psalm 106

1 O give thanks unto the Lord; for He is gracious, * and His mercy endureth for ever.
2 Who can express the noble acts of the Lord, * or show forth all His praise?
3 Blessed are they that alway keep judgment, * and do righteousness.
4 Remember me, O Lord, according to the favor that Thou bearest unto Thy people; * O visit me with Thy salvation;
5 That I may see the felicity of Thy chosen, * and rejoice in the gladness of Thy people, and give thanks with Thine inheritance.
6 We have sinned with our fathers; * we have done amiss, and dealt wickedly.

7 Our fathers regarded not Thy wonders in Egypt, neither kept they Thy great goodness in remembrance; * but were disobedient at the sea, even at the Red Sea.
8 Nevertheless, He helped them for His Name's sake, * that He might make His power to be known.
9 He rebuked the Red Sea also, and it was dried up; * so He led them through the deep, as through a wilderness.
10 And He saved them from the adversary's hand, * and delivered them from the hand of the enemy.
11 As for those that troubled them, the waters overwhelmed them; * there was not one of them left.
12 Then believed they His words, * and sang praise unto Him.
13 But within a while they forgat His works, * and would not abide His counsel.
14 But lust came upon them in the wilderness, * and they tempted God in the desert.
15 And He gave them their desire, * and sent leanness withal into their soul.
16 They angered Moses also in the tents, * and Aaron the saint of the Lord.
17 So the earth opened, and swallowed up Dathan, * and covered the congregation of Abiram.
18 And the fire was kindled in their company; * the flame burnt up the ungodly.
19 They made a calf in Horeb, * and worshiped the molten image.
20 Thus they turned their glory * into the similitude of a calf that eateth hay.
21 And they forgot God their Savior, * Who had done so great things in Egypt;
22 Wondrous works in the land of Ham; * and fearful things by the Red Sea.
23 So He said He would have destroyed them, had not Moses His chosen stood before Him in the gap, * to turn away His wrathful indignation, lest He should destroy them.
24 Yea, they thought scorn of that pleasant land, * and

gave no credence unto His word;

25 But murmured in their tents, * and hearkened not unto the voice of the Lord.

26 Then lift He up His hand against them, * to overthrow them in the wilderness;

27 To cast out their seed among the nations, * and to scatter them in the lands.

28 They joined themselves unto Baal-Peor, * and ate the offerings of the dead.

29 Thus they provoked Him to anger with their own inventions; * and the plague was great among them.

30 Then stood up Phinehas, and interposed; * and so the plague ceased.

31 And that was counted unto Him for righteousness, * among all posterities for evermore.

32 They angered Him also at the waters of strife, * so that He punished Moses for their sakes;

33 Because they provoked His Spirit, * so that he spake unadvisedly with his lips.

34 Neither destroyed they the heathen, * as the Lord commanded them;

35 But were mingled among the heathen, * and learned their works.

36 Insomuch that they worshiped their idols, which became a snare unto them; * yea, they offered their sons and their daughters unto devils;

37 And shed innocent blood, even the blood of their sons and of their daughters, * whom they offered unto the idols of Canaan; and the land was defiled with blood.

38 Thus were they stained with their own works, * and went a whoring with their own inventions.

39 Therefore was the wrath of the Lord kindled against His people, * insomuch that He abhorred His own inheritance.

40 And He gave them over into the hand of the heathen; * and they that hated them were lords over them.

41 Their enemies oppressed them, * and had them in subjection.

42 Many a time did He deliver them; * but they rebelled against Him with their own inventions, and were brought down in their wickedness.
43 Nevertheless, when He saw their adversity, * He heard their complaint.
44 He thought upon His covenant, and pitied them, according unto the multitude of His mercies; * yea, He made all those that led them away captive to pity them.
45 Deliver us, O Lord our God, and gather us from among the heathen; * that we may give thanks unto Thy holy Name, and make our boast of Thy praise.
46 Blessed be the Lord God of Israel, from everlasting, and world without end; * And let all the people say, Amen.

BOOK V

Twenty-second Day

Morning Prayer

Confitemini Domino   Psalm 107

1 O Give thanks unto the Lord, for He is gracious, * and His mercy endureth for ever.
2 Let them give thanks whom the Lord hath redeemed, * and delivered from the hand of the enemy;
3 And gathered them out of the lands, from the east, and from the west; * from the north, and from the south.
4 They went astray in the wilderness out of the way, * and found no city to dwell in.
5 Hungry and thirsty, * their soul fainted in them.
6 So they cried unto the Lord in their trouble, * and He delivered them from their distress.
7 He led them forth by the right way, * that they might go to the city where they dwelt.
8 O that men would therefore praise the Lord for His goodness; * and declare the wonders that He doeth for the children of men!

9 For He satisfieth the empty soul, * and filleth the hungry soul with goodness.

10 Such as sit in darkness, and in the shadow of death, * being fast bound in misery and iron;

11 Because they rebelled against the words of the Lord, * and lightly regarded the counsel of the Most Highest;

12 He also brought down their heart through heaviness: * they fell down, and there was none to help them.

13 So when they cried unto the Lord in their trouble, * He delivered them out of their distress.

14 For He brought them out of darkness, and out of the shadow of death, * and brake their bonds in sunder.

15 O that men would therefore praise the Lord for His goodness; * and declare the wonders that He doeth for the children of men!

16 For He hath broken the gates of brass, * and smitten the bars of iron in sunder.

17 Foolish men are plagued for their offense, * and because of their wickedness.

18 Their soul abhorred all manner of meat, * and they were even hard at death's door.

19 So when they cried unto the Lord in their trouble, * He delivered them out of their distress.

20 He sent His word, and healed them; * and they were saved from their destruction.

21 O that men would therefore praise the Lord for His goodness; * and declare the wonders that He doeth for the children of men!

22 That they would offer unto Him the sacrifice of thanksgiving, * and tell out His works with gladness!

23 They that go down to the sea in ships, * and occupy their business in great waters;

24 These men see the works of the Lord, * and His wonders in the deep.

25 For at His word the stormy wind ariseth, * which lifteth up the waves thereof.

26 They are carried up to the heaven, and down again to

the deep; * their soul melteth away because of the trouble.
27 They reel to and fro, and stagger like a drunken man, *
and are at their wit's end.
28 So when they cry unto the Lord in their trouble, * He
delivereth them out of their distress.
29 For He maketh the storm to cease, * so that the waves
thereof are still.
30 Then are they glad, because they are at rest; * and so
He bringeth them unto the haven where they would be.
31 O that men would therefore praise the Lord for His
goodness; * and declare the wonders that He doeth for the
children of men!
32 That they would exalt Him also in the congregation of
the people, * and praise Him in the seat of the elders!
33 He turneth the floods into a wilderness, * and drieth up
the water-springs.
34 A fruitful land maketh He barren, * for the wickedness of
them that dwell therein.
35 Again, He maketh the wilderness a standing water, * and
water-springs of a dry ground.
36 And there He setteth the hungry, * that they may build
them a city to dwell in;
37 That they may sow their land, and plant vineyards, * to
yield them fruits of increase.
38 He blesseth them, so that they multiply exceedingly; *
and suffereth not their cattle to decrease.
39 And again, when they are minished and brought low *
through oppression, through any plague or trouble;
40 Though He suffer them to be evil entreated through
tyrants, * and let them wander out of the way in the
wilderness;
41 Yet helpeth He the poor out of misery, * and maketh Him
households like a flock of sheep.
42 The righteous will consider this, and rejoice; * and the
mouth of all wickedness shall be stopped.
43 Whoso is wise, will ponder these things; * and they shall
understand the loving-kindness of the Lord.

Evening Prayer

Paratum cor meum   Psalm 108

1 O God, my heart is ready, my heart is ready; * I will sing, and give praise with the best member that I have.
2 Awake, thou lute and harp; * I myself will awake right early.
3 I will give thanks unto Thee, O Lord, among the peoples; * I will sing praises unto Thee among the nations.
4 For Thy mercy is greater than the heavens, * and Thy truth reacheth unto the clouds.
5 Set up Thyself, O God, above the heavens, * and Thy glory above all the earth;
6 That Thy beloved may be delivered: * let Thy right hand save them, and hear Thou me.
7 God hath spoken in His holiness: * "I will rejoice therefore, and divide Shechem, and mete out the Valley of Succoth.
8 Gilead is Mine, and Manasseh is Mine; * Ephraim also is the strength of My head; Judah is My lawgiver;
9 Moab is My wash-pot; over Edom will I cast out My shoe; * upon Philistia will I triumph."
10 Who will lead me into the strong city? * and who will bring me into Edom?
11 Hast not Thou forsaken us, O God? * and wilt not Thou, O God, go forth with our hosts?
12 O help us against the enemy: * for vain is the help of man.
13 Through God we shall do great acts; * and it is He that shall tread down our enemies.

Deus, laudem   Psalm 109

1 Hold not Thy tongue, O God of my praise; * for the mouth of the ungodly, yea, the mouth of the deceitful is opened upon me.

2 And they have spoken against me with false tongues; * they compassed me about also with words of hatred, and fought against me without a cause.

3 For the love that I had unto them, lo, they take now my contrary part; * but I give myself unto prayer.

4 Thus have they rewarded me evil for good, * and hatred for my good will.

5 Set Thou an ungodly man to be ruler over him, * and let an adversary stand at his right hand.

6 When sentence is given upon him, let him be condemned; * and let his prayer be turned into sin.

7 Let his days be few; * and let another take his office.

8 Let his children be fatherless, * and his wife a widow.

9 Let his children be vagabonds, and beg their bread; * let them seek it also out of desolate places.

10 Let the extortioner consume all that he hath; * and let the stranger spoil his labor.

11 Let there be no man to pity him, * nor to have compassion upon his fatherless children.

12 Let his posterity be destroyed; * and in the next generation let his name be clean put out.

13 Let the wickedness of his fathers be had in remembrance in the sight of the Lord; * and let not the sin of his mother be done away.

14 Let them alway be before the Lord, * that He may root out the memorial of them from off the earth;

15 And that, because his mind was not to do good; * but persecuted the poor helpless man, that he might slay him that was vexed at the heart.

16 His delight was in cursing, and it shall happen unto him; * he loved not blessing, therefore shall it be far from him.

17 He clothed himself with cursing like as with a raiment, * and it shall come into his bowels like water, and like oil into his bones.

18 Let it be unto him as the cloak that he hath upon him, * and as the girdle that he is alway girded withal.

19 Let it thus happen from the Lord unto mine enemies, *

and to those that speak evil against my soul.
20 But deal Thou with me, O Lord God, according unto Thy Name; * for sweet is Thy mercy.
21 O deliver me, for I am helpless and poor, * and my heart is wounded within me.
22 I go hence like the shadow that departeth, * and am driven away as the grasshopper.
23 My knees are weak through fasting; * my flesh is dried up for want of fatness.
24 I am become also a reproach unto them: * they that look upon me shake their heads.
25 Help me, O Lord my God; * O save me according to Thy mercy;
26 And they shall know how that this is Thy hand, * and that Thou, Lord, hast done it.
27 Though they curse, yet bless Thou; * and let them be confounded that rise up against me; but let Thy servant rejoice.
28 Let mine adversaries be clothed with shame; * and let them cover themselves with their own confusion, as with a cloak.
29 As for me, I will give great thanks unto the Lord with my mouth, * and praise Him among the multitude;
30 For he shall stand at the right hand of the poor, * to save his soul from unrighteous judges.

Twenty-third Day

Morning Prayer

Dixit Dominus   Psalm 110

1 The Lord said unto my Lord, * "Sit Thou on my right hand, until I make Thine enemies Thy footstool."
2 The Lord shall send the rod of Thy power out of Zion: * be Thou ruler, even in the midst among Thine enemies.
3 In the day of Thy power shall Thy people offer themselves willingly with an holy worship: * Thy young men come to

Thee as dew from the womb of the morning.
4 The Lord sware, and will not repent, * "Thou art a Priest for ever after the order of Melchizedek."
5 The Lord upon Thy right hand * shall wound even kings in the day of His wrath.
6 He shall judge among the heathen; * He shall fill the places with the dead bodies, and smite in sunder the heads over divers countries.
7 He shall drink of the brook in the way; * therefore shall He lift up His head.

Confitebor tibi   Psalm 111

1 I will give thanks unto the Lord with my whole heart, * secretly among the faithful, and in the congregation.
2 The works of the Lord are great, * sought out of all them that have pleasure therein.
3 His work is worthy to be praised and had in honor, * and His righteousness endureth for ever.
4 The merciful and gracious Lord hath so done His marvelous works, * that they ought to be had in remembrance.
5 He hath given meat unto them that fear Him; * He shall ever be mindful of His covenant.
6 He hath showed His people the power of His works, * that He may give them the heritage of the heathen.
7 The works of His hands are verity and judgment; * all His commandments are true.
8 They stand fast for ever and ever, * and are done in truth and equity.
9 He sent redemption unto His people; * He hath commanded His covenant for ever; holy and reverend is His Name.
10 The fear of the Lord is the beginning of wisdom; * a good understanding have all they that do thereafter; His praise endureth for ever.

1 Blessed is the man that feareth the Lord; * he hath great delight in His commandments.

2 His seed shall be mighty upon earth; * the generation of the faithful shall be blessed.

3 Riches and plenteousness shall be in his house; * and his righteousness endureth for ever.

4 Unto the godly there ariseth up light in the darkness; * he is merciful, loving, and righteous.

5 A good man is merciful, and lendeth; * and will guide his words with discretion.

6 For he shall never be moved: * and the righteous shall be had in everlasting remembrance.

7 He will not be afraid of any evil tidings; * for his heart standeth fast, and believeth in the Lord.

8 His heart is established, and will not shrink, * until he see his desire upon his enemies.

9 He hath dispersed abroad, and given to the poor. * and his righteousness remaineth for ever; his horn shall be exalted with honor.

10 The ungodly shall see it, and it shall grieve him; * he shall gnash with his teeth, and consume away; the desire of the ungodly shall perish.

Laudate, pueri   Psalm 113

1 Praise the Lord, ye servants; * O praise the Name of the Lord.

2 Blessed be the Name of the Lord * from this time forth for evermore.

3 The Lord's Name is praised * from the rising up of the sun unto the going down of the same.

4 The Lord is high above all nations, * and His glory above the heavens.

5 Who is like unto the Lord our God, that hath His dwelling so high, * and yet humbleth Himself to behold the things that are in heaven and earth!

6 He taketh up the simple out of the dust, * and lifteth the poor out of the mire;
7 That He may set him with the princes, * even with the princes of His people.
8 He maketh the barren woman to keep house, * and to be a joyful mother of children.

Evening Prayer

In exitu Israel   Psalm 114

1 When Israel came out of Egypt, * and the house of Jacob from among the strange people,
2 Judah was His sanctuary, * and Israel His dominion.
3 The sea saw that, and fled; * Jordan was driven back.
4 The mountains skipped like rams, * and the little hills like young sheep.
5 What aileth thee, O thou sea, that thou fleddest? * and thou Jordan, that thou wast driven back?
6 Ye mountains, that ye skipped like rams? * and ye little hills, like young sheep?
7 Tremble, thou earth, at the presence of the Lord: * at the presence of the God of Jacob;
8 Who turned the hard rock into a standing water, * and the flint-stone into a springing well.

Non nobis, Domine   Psalm 115

1 Not unto us, O Lord, not unto us, but unto Thy Name give the praise; * for Thy loving mercy, and for Thy truth's sake.
2 Wherefore shall the heathen say, * "Where is now their God?"
3 As for our God, He is in heaven: * He hath done whatsoever pleased Him.
4 Their idols are silver and gold, * even the work of men's hands.
5 They have mouths, and speak not; * eyes have they, and see not.

6 They have ears, and hear not; * noses have they, and smell not.
7 They have hands, and handle not; feet have they, and walk not; * neither speak they through their throat.
8 They that make them are like unto them; * and so are all such as put their trust in them.
9 But thou, house of Israel, trust thou in the Lord; * He is their helper and defender.
10 Ye house of Aaron, put your trust in the Lord; * He is their helper and defender.
11 Ye that fear the Lord, put your trust in the Lord; * He is their helper and defender.
12 The Lord hath been mindful of us, and He shall bless us; * even He shall bless the house of Israel, He shall bless the house of Aaron.
13 He shall bless them that fear the Lord, * both small and great.
14 The Lord shall increase you more and more, * you and your children.
15 Ye are the blessed of the Lord, * Who made heaven and earth.
16 All the whole heavens are the Lord's; * the earth hath He given to the children of men.
17 The dead praise not Thee, O Lord, * neither all they that go down into silence.
18 But we will praise the Lord, * from this time forth for evermore. Praise the Lord.

Twenty-fourth Day

Morning Prayer

Dilexi, quoniam   Psalm 116

1 My delight is in the Lord; * because He hath heard the voice of my prayer;
2 Because He hath inclined his ear unto me; * therefore will I call upon Him as long as I live.

3 The snares of death compassed me round about, * and the pains of hell gat hold upon me.
4 I found trouble and heaviness; then called I upon the Name of the Lord; * "O Lord, I beseech Thee, deliver my soul."
5 Gracious is the Lord, and righteous; * yea, our God is merciful.
6 The Lord preserveth the simple: * I was in misery, and He helped me.
7 Turn again then unto Thy rest, O my soul; * for the Lord hath rewarded Thee.
8 And why? Thou hast delivered my soul from death, * mine eyes from tears, and my feet from falling.
9 I will walk before the Lord * in the land of the living.
10 I believed, and therefore will I speak; but I was sore troubled: * I said in my haste, "All men are liars."
11 What reward shall I give unto the Lord * for all the benefits that He hath done unto me?
12 I will receive the cup of salvation, * and call upon the Name of the Lord.
13 I will pay my vows now in the presence of all His people: * right dear in the sight of the Lord is the death of His saints.
14 Behold, O Lord, how that I am Thy servant; * I am Thy servant, and the son of Thine handmaid; Thou hast broken my bonds in sunder.
15 I will offer to Thee the sacrifice of thanksgiving, * and will call upon the Name of the Lord.
16 I will pay my vows unto the Lord, in the sight of all His people, * in the courts of the Lord's house; even in the midst of thee, O Jerusalem. Praise the Lord.

Laudate Dominum   Psalm 117

1 O praise the Lord, all ye nations; * praise Him, all ye peoples.
2 For His merciful kindness is ever more and more toward us; * and the truth of the Lord endureth for ever. Praise the Lord.

1 O give thanks unto the Lord, for He is gracious; * because His mercy endureth for ever.

2 Let Israel now confess that He is gracious, * and that His mercy endureth for ever.

3 Let the house of Aaron now confess, * that His mercy endureth for ever.

4 Yea, let them now that fear the Lord confess, * that His mercy endureth for ever.

5 I called upon the Lord in trouble; * and the Lord heard me at large.

6 The Lord is on my side; * I will not fear what man doeth unto me.

7 The Lord taketh my part with them that help me; * therefore shall I see my desire upon mine enemies.

8 It is better to trust in the Lord, * than to put any confidence in man.

9 It is better to trust in the Lord, * than to put any confidence in princes.

10 All nations compassed me round about; * but in the Name of the Lord will I destroy them.

11 They kept me in on every side, they kept me in, I say, on every side; * but in the Name of the Lord will I destroy them.

12 They came about me like bees, and are extinct even as the fire among the thorns; * for in the Name of the Lord I will destroy them.

13 Thou hast thrust sore at me, that I might fall; * but the Lord was my help.

14 The Lord is my strength, and my song; * and is become my salvation.

15 The voice of joy and health is in the dwellings of the righteous; * the right hand of the Lord bringeth mighty things to pass.

16 The right hand of the Lord hath the pre-eminence; * the right hand of the Lord bringeth mighty things to pass.

17 I shall not die, but live, * and declare the works of the Lord.
18 The Lord hath chastened and corrected me; * but He hath not given me over unto death.
19 Open me the gates of righteousness, * that I may go into them, and give thanks unto the Lord.
20 This is the gate of the Lord, * the righteous shall enter into it.
21 I will thank Thee; for Thou hast heard me, * and art become my salvation.
22 The same stone which the builders refused, * is become the head-stone in the comer.
23 This is the Lord's doing, * and it is marvelous in our eyes.
24 This is the day which the Lord hath made; * we will rejoice and be glad in it.
25 Help me now, O Lord: * O Lord, send us now prosperity.
26 Blessed be he that cometh in the Name of the Lord: * we have wished you good luck, we that are of the house of the Lord.
27 God is the Lord, Who hath showed us light: * bind the sacrifice with cords, yea, even unto the horns of the altar.
28 Thou art my God, and I will thank Thee; * Thou art my God, and I will praise Thee.
29 O give thanks unto the Lord; for He is gracious, * and His mercy endureth for ever.

Evening Prayer

Beati immaculati   Psalm 119. Aleph

1 Blessed are those that are undefiled in the way, and walk in the law of the Lord.
2 Blessed are they that keep his testimonies, * and seek him with their whole heart;
3 Even they who do no wickedness, * and walk in his ways.
4 Thou hast charged * that we shall diligently keep thy commandments.

5 O that my ways were made so direct, * that I might keep thy statutes!
6 So shall I not be confounded, * while I have respect unto all thy commandments.
7 I will thank thee with an unfeigned heart, * when I shall have learned the judgments of thy righteousness.
8 I will keep thy statutes; * O forsake me not utterly.

In quo corrigit?   Beth

9 Wherewithal shall a young man cleanse his way? * even by ruling himself after thy word.
10 With my whole heart have I sought thee; * O let me not go wrong out of thy commandments.
11 Thy word have I hid within my heart, * that I should not sin against thee.
12 Blessed art thou, O Lord; * O teach me thy statutes.
13 With my lips have I been telling * of all the judgments of thy mouth.
14 I have had as great delight in the way of thy testimonies, * as in all manner of riches.
15 I will talk of thy commandments, * and have respect unto thy ways.
16 My delight shall be in thy statutes, * and I will not forget thy word.

Retribue servo tuo   Gimel

17 O do well unto thy servant; * that I may live, and keep thy word.
18 Open thou mine eyes; * that I may see the wondrous things of thy law.
19 I am a stranger upon earth; * O hide not thy commandments from me.
20 My soul breaketh out for the very fervent desire * that it hath alway unto thy judgments.
21 Thou hast rebuked the proud; * and cursed are they that do err from thy commandments.

22 O turn from me shame and rebuke; * for I have kept thy testimonies.
23 Princes also did sit and speak against me; * but thy servant is occupied in thy statutes.
24 For thy testimonies are my delight, * and my counselors.

Adhaesit pavimento   Daleth

25 My soul cleaveth to the dust; * O quicken thou me, according to thy word.
26 I have acknowledged my ways, and thou heardest me: * O teach me thy statutes.
27 Make me to understand the way of thy commandments; * and so shall I talk of thy wondrous works.
28 My soul melteth away for very heaviness; * comfort thou me according unto thy word.
29 Take from me the way of lying, * and cause thou me to make much of thy law.
30 I have chosen the way of truth, * and thy judgments have I laid before me.
31 I have stuck unto thy testimonies; * O Lord, confound me not.
32 I will run the way of thy commandments, * when thou hast set my heart at liberty.

Twenty-fifth Day

Morning Prayer

Legem pone   He

33 Teach me, O Lord, the way of Thy statutes, * and I shall keep it unto the end.
34 Give me understanding, and I shall keep Thy law; * yea, I shall keep it with my whole heart.
35 Make me to go in the path of Thy commandments; * for therein is my desire.
36 Incline my heart unto Thy testimonies, * and not to

covetousness.
37 O turn away mine eyes, lest they behold vanity; * and quicken Thou me in Thy way.
38 O establish Thy word in Thy servant, * that I may fear Thee.
39 Take away the rebuke that I am afraid of; * for Thy judgments are good.
40 Behold, my delight is in Thy commandments; * O quicken me in Thy righteousness.

Et veniat super me   Waw

41 Let Thy loving mercy come also unto me, O Lord, * even Thy salvation, according unto Thy word.
42 So shall I make answer unto my blasphemers; * for my trust is in Thy word.
43 O take not the word of Thy truth utterly out of my mouth; * for my hope is in Thy judgments.
44 So shall I alway keep Thy law; * yea, for ever and ever.
45 And I will walk at liberty; * for I seek Thy commandments.
46 I will speak of Thy testimonies also, even before kings, * and will not be ashamed.
47 And my delight shall be in Thy commandments, * which I have loved.
48 My hands also will I lift up unto Thy commandments, which I have loved; * and my study shall be in Thy statutes.

Memor esto verbi tui   Zayin

49 O think upon Thy servant, as concerning Thy word, * wherein Thou hast caused me to put my trust.
50 The same is my comfort in my trouble; * for Thy word hath quickened me.
51 The proud have had me exceedingly in derision; * yet have I not shrinked from Thy law.
52 For I remembered Thine everlasting judgments, O Lord, * and received comfort.

53 I am horribly afraid, * for the ungodly that forsake Thy law.
54 Thy statutes have been my songs, * in the house of my pilgrimage.
55 I have thought upon Thy Name, O Lord, in the night season, * and have kept Thy law.
56 This I had, * because I kept Thy commandments.

Portio mea, Domine   Heth

57 Thou art my portion, O Lord; * I have promised to keep Thy law.
58 I made my humble petition in Thy presence with my whole heart; * O be merciful unto me, according to Thy word.
59 I called mine own ways to remembrance, * and turned my feet unto Thy testimonies.
60 I made haste, and prolonged not the time, * to keep Thy commandments.
61 The snares of the ungodly have compassed me about; * but I have not forgotten Thy law.
62 At midnight I will rise to give thanks unto Thee, * because of Thy righteous judgments.
63 I am a companion of all them that fear Thee, * and keep Thy commandments.
64 The earth, O Lord, is full of Thy mercy: * O teach me Thy statutes.

Bonitatem fecisti   Teth

65 O Lord, Thou hast dealt graciously with Thy servant, * according unto Thy word.
66 O teach me true understanding and knowledge; * for I have believed Thy commandments.
67 Before I was troubled, I went wrong; * but now have I kept Thy word.
68 Thou art good and gracious; * O teach me Thy statutes.
69 The proud have imagined a lie against me; * but I will

keep Thy commandments with my whole heart.

70 Their heart is as fat as brawn; * but my delight hath been in Thy law.

71 It is good for me that I have been in trouble; * that I may learn Thy statutes.

72 The law of Thy mouth is dearer unto me * than thousands of gold and silver.

Evening Prayer

Manus tuae fecerunt me   Yod

73 Thy hands have made me and fashioned me: * O give me understanding, that I may learn Thy commandments.

74 They that fear Thee will be glad when they see me; * because I have put my trust in Thy word.

75 I know, O Lord, that Thy judgments are right, * and that Thou of very faithfulness hast caused me to be troubled.

76 O let Thy merciful kindness be my comfort, * according to Thy word unto Thy servant.

77 O let Thy loving mercies come unto me, that I may live; * for Thy law is my delight.

78 Let the proud be confounded, for they go wickedly about to destroy me; * but I will be occupied in Thy commandments.

79 Let such as fear Thee, and have known Thy testimonies, * be turned unto me.

80 O let my heart be sound in Thy statutes, * that I be not ashamed.

Defecit anima mea   Kaph

81 MY soul hath longed for Thy salvation, * and I have a good hope because of Thy word.

82 Mine eyes-long sore for Thy word; * saying, "O when wilt Thou comfort me?"

83 For I am become like a bottle in the smoke; * yet do I not forget Thy statutes.

84 How many are the days of Thy servant? * when wilt Thou be avenged of them that persecute me?
85 The proud have digged pits for me, * which are not after Thy law.
86 All Thy commandments are true: * they persecute me falsely; O be Thou my help.
87 They had almost made an end of me upon earth; * but I forsook not Thy commandments.
88 O quicken me after Thy loving-kindness; * and so shall I keep the testimonies of Thy mouth.

In aeternum, Domine   Lamed

90 O Lord, Thy word * endureth for ever in heaven. Thy truth also remaineth from one generation to another; * Thou hast laid the foundation of the earth, and it abideth.
91 They continue this day according to Thine ordinance; * for all things serve Thee.
92 If my delight had not been in Thy law, * I should have perished in my trouble.
93 I will never forget Thy commandments; * for with them Thou hast quickened me.
94 I am Thine: O save me, * for I have sought Thy commandments.
95 The ungodly laid wait for me, to destroy me; * but I will consider Thy testimonies.
96 I see that all things come to an end; * but Thy commandment is exceeding broad.

Quomodo dilexi!   Mem

97 Lord, what love have I unto Thy law! * all the day long is my study in it.
98 Thou, through Thy commandments, hast made me wiser than mine enemies; * for they are ever with me.
99 I have more understanding than my teachers; * for Thy testimonies are my study.
100 I am wiser than the aged; * because I keep Thy

commandments.

101 I have refrained my feet from every evil way, * that I may keep Thy word.

102 I have not shrunk from Thy judgments; * for Thou teachest me.

103 O how sweet are Thy words unto my throat; * yea, sweeter than honey unto my mouth!

104 Through Thy commandments I get understanding: * therefore I hate all evil ways.

Twenty-sixth Day

Morning Prayer

Lucerna pedibus meis   Nun

105 Thy word is a lantern unto my feet, * and a light unto my paths.

106 I have sworn, and am steadfastly purposed, * to keep Thy righteous judgments.

107 I am troubled above measure: * quicken me, O Lord, according to Thy word.

108 Let the free-will offerings of my mouth please Thee, O Lord; * and teach me Thy judgments.

109 My soul is alway in my hand; * yet do I not forget Thy law.

110 The ungodly have laid a snare for me; * but yet I swerved not from Thy commandments.

111 Thy testimonies have I claimed as mine heritage for ever; * and why? they are the very joy of my heart.

112 I have applied my heart to fulfill Thy statutes alway, * even unto the end.

Iniquos odio habui   Samek

113 I Hate them that imagine evil things; * but Thy law do I love.

114 Thou art my defense and shield; * and my trust is in

178

Thy word.
115 Away from me, ye wicked; * I will keep the commandments of my God.
116 O establish me according to Thy word, that I may live; * and let me not be disappointed of my hope.
117 Hold Thou me up, and I shall be safe; * yea, my delight shall be ever in Thy statutes.
118 Thou hast trodden down all them that depart from Thy statutes; * for they imagine but deceit.
119 Thou puttest away all the ungodly of the earth like dross; * therefore I love Thy testimonies.
120 My flesh trembleth for fear of Thee; * and I am afraid of Thy judgments.

Feci judicium   Ayin

121 I deal with the thing that is lawful and right; * O give me not over unto mine oppressors.
122 Make Thou Thy servant to delight in that which is good, * that the proud do me no wrong.
123 Mine eyes are wasted away with looking for Thy health, * and for the word of Thy righteousness.
124 O deal with Thy servant according unto Thy loving mercy, * and teach me Thy statutes.
125 I am Thy servant; O grant me understanding, * that I may know Thy testimonies.
126 It is time for Thee, Lord, to lay to Thine hand; * for they have destroyed Thy law.
127 For I love Thy commandments * above gold and precious stones.
128 Therefore hold I straight all Thy commandments; * and all false ways I utterly abhor.

Mirabilia   Pe

129 Thy testimonies are wonderful; * therefore doth my soul keep them.
130 When Thy word goeth forth, * it giveth light and

understanding unto the simple.

131 I opened my mouth, and drew in my breath; * for my delight was in Thy commandments.

132 O look Thou upon me, and be merciful unto me, * as Thou usest to do unto those that love Thy Name.

133 Order my steps in Thy word; * and so shall no wickedness have dominion over me.

134 O deliver me from the wrongful dealings of men; * and so shall I keep Thy commandments.

135 Show the light of Thy countenance upon Thy servant, * and teach me Thy statutes.

136 Mine eyes gush out with water, * because men keep not Thy law.

Justus es, Domine Tsadde

137 Righteous art Thou, O Lord; * and true are Thy judgments.

138 The testimonies that Thou hast commanded * are exceeding righteous and true.

139 My zeal hath even consumed me; * because mine enemies have forgotten Thy words.

140 Thy word is tried to the uttermost, * and Thy servant loveth it.

141 I am small and of no reputation; * yet do I not forget Thy commandments.

142 Thy righteousness is an everlasting righteousness, * and Thy law is the truth.

143 Trouble and heaviness have taken hold upon me; * yet is my delight in Thy commandments.

144 The righteousness of Thy testimonies is everlasting: * O grant me understanding, and I shall live.

Evening Prayer

Clamavi in toto corde meo Qoph

145 I call with my whole heart; * hear me, O Lord; I will keep

Thy statutes.
146 Yea, even unto Thee do I call; * help me, and I shall keep Thy testimonies.
147 Early in the morning do I cry unto Thee; * for in Thy word is my trust.
148 Mine eyes prevent the night watches; * that I might be occupied in Thy word.
149 Hear my voice, O Lord, according unto Thy lovingkindness; * quicken me, according to Thy judgments.
150 They draw nigh that of malice persecute me, * and are far from Thy law.
151 Be Thou nigh at hand, O Lord; * for all Thy commandments are true.
152 As concerning Thy testimonies, I have known long since, * that Thou hast grounded them for ever.

Vide humilitatem   Resh

153 O consider mine adversity, and deliver me, * for I do not forget Thy law.
154 Avenge Thou my cause, and deliver me; * quicken me according to Thy word.
155 Health is far from the ungodly; * for they regard not Thy statutes.
156 Great is Thy mercy, O Lord; * quicken me, as Thou art wont.
157 Many there are that trouble me, and persecute me; * yet do I not swerve from Thy testimonies.
158 It grieveth me when I see the transgressors; * because they keep not Thy law.
159 Consider, O Lord, how I love Thy commandments; * O quicken me, according to Thy loving-kindness.
160 Thy word is true from everlasting; * all the judgments of Thy righteousness endure for evermore.

161 Princes have persecuted me without a cause; * but my heart standeth in awe of Thy word.
162 I am as glad of Thy word, * as one that findeth great spoils.
163 As for lies, I hate and abhor them; * but Thy law do I love.
164 Seven times a day do I praise Thee; * because of Thy righteous judgments.
165 Great is the peace that they have who love Thy law; * and they have none occasion of stumbling.
166 Lord, I have looked for Thy saving health, * and done after Thy commandments.
167 My soul hath kept Thy testimonies, * and loved them exceedingly.
168 I have kept Thy commandments and testimonies; * for all my ways are before Thee.

Appropinquet deprecatio   Tau

169 Let my complaint come before Thee, O Lord; * give me understanding according to Thy word.
170 Let my supplication come before Thee; * deliver me according to Thy word.
171 My lips shall speak of Thy praise, * when Thou hast taught me Thy statutes.
172 Yea, my tongue shall sing of Thy word; * for all Thy commandments are righteous.
173 Let Thine hand help me; * for I have chosen Thy commandments.
174 I have longed for Thy saving health, O Lord; * and in Thy law is my delight.
175 O let my soul live, and it shall praise Thee; * and Thy judgments shall help me.
176 I have gone astray like a sheep that is lost; * O seek Thy servant, for I do not forget Thy commandments.

Twenty-seventh Day

Morning Prayer

Ad Dominum   Psalm 120

1 When I was in trouble, I called upon the Lord, * and He heard me.
2 Deliver my soul, O Lord, from lying lips, * and from a deceitful tongue.
3 What reward shall be given or done unto thee, thou false tongue? * even mighty and sharp arrows, with hot burning coals.
4 Woe is me, that I am constrained to dwell with Meshech, * and to have my habitation among the tents of Kedar!
5 My soul hath long dwelt among them * that are enemies unto peace.
6 I labor for peace; but when I speak unto them thereof, * they make them ready to battle.

Levavi oculos   Psalm 121

1 I will lift up mine eyes unto the hills; * from whence cometh my help?
2 My help cometh even from the Lord, * Who hath made heaven and earth.
3 He will not suffer thy foot to be moved; * and He that keepeth thee will not sleep.
4 Behold, He that keepeth Israel * shall neither slumber nor sleep.
5 The Lord Himself is thy keeper; * the Lord is thy defense upon thy right hand;
6 So that the sun shall not burn thee by day, * neither the moon by night.
7 The Lord shall preserve thee from all evil; * yea, it is even He that shall keep thy soul.
8 The Lord shall preserve thy going out, and thy coming in, * from this time forth for evermore.

Laetatus sum   Psalm 122

1 I was glad when they said unto me, * "We will go into the house of the Lord."
2 Our feet shall stand in thy gates, * O Jerusalem.
3 Jerusalem is built as a city * that is at unity in itself.
4 For thither the tribes go up, even the tribes of the Lord, * to testify unto Israel, to give thanks unto the Name of the Lord.
5 For there is the seat of judgment, * even the seat of the house of David.
6 O pray for the peace of Jerusalem; * they shall prosper that love thee.
7 Peace be within thy walls, * and plenteousness within thy palaces.
8 For my brethren and companions' sakes, * I will wish thee prosperity.
9 Yea, because of the house of the Lord our God, * I will seek to do thee good.

Ad te levavi oculos meos   Psalm 123

1 Unto Thee lift I up mine eyes, * O Thou that dwellest in the heavens.
2 Behold, even as the eyes of servants look unto the hand of their masters, and as the eyes of a maiden unto the hand of her mistress, * even so our eyes wait upon the Lord our God, until He have mercy upon us.
3 Have mercy upon us, O Lord, have mercy upon us; * for we are utterly despised.
4 Our soul is filled with the scornful reproof of the wealthy, * and with the spitefulness of the proud.

Nisi quia Dominus   Psalm 124

1 "If the Lord Himself had not been on our side," now may Israel say; * "if the Lord Himself had not been on our side,

when men rose up against us;
2 They had swallowed us up alive; * when they were so wrathfully displeased at us.
3 Yea, the waters had drowned us, * and the stream had gone over our soul.
4 The deep waters of the proud * had gone even over our soul."
5 But praised be the Lord, * Who hath not given us over for a prey unto their teeth.
6 Our soul is escaped even as a bird out of the snare of the fowler; * the snare is broken, and we are delivered.
7 Our help standeth in the Name of the Lord, * Who hath made heaven and earth.

Qui confidunt   Psalm 125

1 They that put their trust in the Lord shall be even as the Mount Zion, * which may not be removed, but standeth fast for ever.
2 The hills stand about Jerusalem; * even so standeth the Lord round about His people, from this time forth for evermore.
3 For the scepter of the ungodly shall not abide upon the lot of the righteous; * lest the righteous put their hand unto wickedness.
4 Do well, O Lord, * unto those that are good and true of heart.
5 As for such as turn back unto their own wickedness, * the Lord shall lead them forth with the evil doers; but peace shall be upon Israel.

Evening Prayer

In convertendo   Psalm 126

1 When the Lord turned again the captivity of Zion, then were we like unto them that dream.
2 Then was our mouth filled with laughter, * and our tongue

with joy.
3 Then said they among the heathen, * "The Lord hath done great things for them."
4 Yea, the Lord hath done great things for us already; * whereof we rejoice.
5 Turn our captivity, O Lord, * as the rivers in the south.
6 They that sow in tears * shall reap in joy.
7 He that now goeth on his way weeping, and beareth forth good seed, * shall doubtless come again with joy, and bring his sheaves with him.

Nisi Dominus   Psalm 127

1 Except the Lord build the house, * their labor is but lost that build it.
2 Except the Lord keep the city, * the watchman waketh but in vain.
3 It is but lost labor that ye haste to rise up early, and so late take rest, and eat the bread of carefulness; * for so He giveth His beloved sleep.
4 Lo, children, and the fruit of the womb, * are an heritage and gift that cometh of the Lord.
5 Like as the arrows in the hand of the giant, * even so are the young children.
6 Happy is the man that hath his quiver full of them; * they shall not be ashamed when they speak with their enemies in the gate.

Beati omnes   Psalm 128

1 Blessed are all they that fear the Lord, * and walk in His ways.
2 For thou shalt eat the labors of thine hands: * O well is thee, and happy shalt thou be.
3 Thy wife shall be as the fruitful vine * upon the walls of thine house;
4 Thy children like the olive-branches * round about thy table.

5 Lo, thus shall the man be blessed * that feareth the Lord.
6 The Lord from out of Zion shall so bless thee, * that thou shalt see Jerusalem in prosperity all thy life long;
7 Yea, that thou shalt see thy children's children, * and peace upon Israel.

Saepe expugnaverunt   Psalm 129

1 "Many a time have they fought against me from my youth up," * may Israel now say;
2 "Yea, many a time have they vexed me from my youth up; * but they have not prevailed against me.
3 The plowers plowed upon my back, * and made long furrows."
4 But the righteous Lord * hath hewn the snares of the ungodly in pieces.
5 Let them be confounded and turned backward, * as many as have evil will at Zion.
6 Let them be even as the grass upon the housetops, * which withereth afore it be grown up;
7 Whereof the mower filleth not his hand, * neither he that bindeth up the sheaves his bosom.
8 So that they who go by say not so much as, "The Lord prosper you; * we wish you good luck in the Name of the Lord."

De profundis   Psalm 130

1 Out of the deep have I called unto Thee, O Lord; * Lord, hear my voice.
2 O let Thine ears consider well * the voice of my complaint.
3 If Thou, Lord, wilt be extreme to mark what is done amiss, * O Lord, who may abide it?
4 For there is mercy with Thee; * therefore shalt Thou be feared.
5 I look for the Lord; my soul doth wait for Him; * in His word is my trust.

6 My soul fleeth unto the Lord before the morning watch; * I say, before the morning watch.
7 O Israel, trust in the Lord; for with the Lord there is mercy, * and with Him is plenteous redemption.
8 And He shall redeem Israel * from all his sins.

Domine, non est   Psalm 131

1 Lord, I am not high-minded; * I have no proud looks.
2 I do not exercise myself in great matters * which are too high for me.
3 But I refrain my soul, and keep it low, like as a child that is weaned from his mother: * yea, my soul is even as a weaned child.
4 O Israel, trust in the Lord * from this time forth for evermore.

Twenty-eighth Day

Morning Prayer

Memento, Domine   Psalm 132

1 Lord, remember David, * and all his trouble:
2 How he swore unto the Lord, * and vowed a vow unto the Almighty God of Jacob:
3 "I will not come within the tabernacle of mine house, * nor climb up into my bed;
4 I will not suffer mine eyes to sleep, nor mine eyelids to slumber; * neither the temples of my head to take any rest;
5 Until I find out a place for the temple of the Lord; * an habitation for the Mighty God of Jacob."
6 Lo, we heard of the same at Ephratah, * and found it in the wood.
7 We will go into His tabernacle, * and fall low on our knees before His footstool.
8 Arise, O Lord, into Thy resting-place; * Thou, and the ark

of Thy strength.

9 Let Thy priests be clothed with righteousness; * and let Thy saints sing with joyfulness.

10 For Thy servant David's sake, * turn not away the face of Thine anointed.

11 The Lord hath made a faithful oath unto David, * and He shall not shrink from it:

12 "Of the fruit of thy body * shall I set upon thy throne.

13 If thy children will keep My covenant, and My testimonies that I shall teach them; * their children also shall sit upon thy throne for evermore."

14 For the Lord hath chosen Zion to be an habitation for Himself; * He hath longed for her.

15 "This shall be My rest for ever: * here will I dwell, for I have a delight therein.

16 I will bless her victuals with increase, * and will satisfy her poor with bread.

17 I will deck her priests with health, * and her saints shall rejoice and sing.

18 There shall I make the horn of David to flourish: * I have ordained a lantern for mine anointed.

19 As for his enemies, I shall clothe them with shame; * but upon himself shall his crown flourish."

Ecce, quam bonum!   Psalm 133

1 Behold, how good and joyful a thing it is, * for brethren to dwell together in unity!

2 It is like the precious oil upon the head, that ran down unto the beard, * even unto Aaron's beard, and went down to the skirts of his clothing.

3 Like as the dew of Hermon, * which fell upon the hill of Zion.

4 For there the Lord promised His blessing, * and life for evermore.

Ecce nunc   Psalm 134

1 Behold now, praise the Lord, * all ye servants of the Lord;
2 Ye that by night stand in the house of the Lord, * even in
the courts of the house of our God.
3 Lift up your hands in the sanctuary, * and praise the Lord.
4 The Lord that made heaven and earth * give thee
blessing out of Zion.

Laudate Nomen   Psalm 135

1 O praise the Lord, laud ye the Name of the Lord; * praise
it, O ye servants of the Lord;
2 Ye that stand in the house of the Lord, * in the courts of
the house of our God.
3 O praise the Lord, for the Lord is gracious; * O sing
praises unto His Name, for it is lovely.
4 For why? the Lord hath chosen Jacob unto Himself, * and
Israel for His own possession.
5 For I know that the Lord is great, * and that our Lord is
above all gods.
6 Whatsoever the Lord pleased, that did He in heaven, and
in earth; * and in the sea, and in all deep places.
7 He bringeth forth the clouds from the ends of the world, *
and sendeth forth lightnings with the rain, bringing the
winds out of His treasuries.
8 He smote the firstborn of Egypt, * both of man and beast.
9 He hath sent tokens and wonders into the midst of thee,
O thou land of Egypt; * upon Pharaoh, and all his servants.
10 He smote divers nations, * and slew mighty kings:
11 Sihon, king of the Amorites; and Og, the king of Bashan;
* and all the kingdoms of Canaan;
12 And gave their land to be an heritage, * even an heritage
unto Israel His people.
13 Thy Name, O Lord, endureth for ever; * so doth Thy
memorial, O Lord, from one generation to another.
14 For the Lord will avenge His people, * and be gracious

unto His servants.

15 As for the images of the heathen, they are but silver and gold; * the work of men's hands.

16 They have mouths, and speak not; * eyes have they, but they see not.

17 They have ears, and yet they hear not; * neither is there any breath in their mouths.

18 They that make them are like unto them; * and so are all they that put their trust in them.

19 Praise the Lord, ye house of Israel; * praise the Lord, ye house of Aaron.

20 Praise the Lord, ye house of Levi; * ye that fear the Lord, praise the Lord.

21 Praised be the Lord out of Zion, * Who dwelleth at Jerusalem.

Evening Prayer

Confitemini   Psalm 136

1 O give thanks unto the Lord, for He is gracious: * and His mercy endureth for ever.

2 O give thanks unto the God of all gods: * for His mercy endureth for ever.

3 O thank the Lord of all lords: * for His mercy endureth for ever.

4 Who only doeth great wonders: * for His mercy endureth for ever.

5 Who by His excellent wisdom made the heavens: for His mercy endureth for ever.

6 Who laid out the earth above the waters: * for His mercy endureth for ever.

7 Who hath made great lights: * for His mercy endureth for ever:

8 The sun to rule the day: * for His mercy endureth for ever;

9 The moon and the stars to govern the night: * for His mercy endureth for ever.

10 Who smote Egypt, with their firstborn: * for His mercy endureth for ever;
11 And brought out Israel from among them: * for His mercy endureth for ever;
12 With a mighty hand and stretched-out arm: * for His mercy endureth for ever.
13 Who divided the Red Sea in two parts: * for His mercy endureth for ever;
14 And made Israel to go through the midst of it: * for His mercy endureth for ever.
15 But as for Pharaoh and his host, he overthrew them in the Red Sea: * for His mercy endureth for ever.
16 Who led His people through the wilderness: * for His mercy endureth for ever.
17 Who smote great kings: * for His mercy endureth for ever;
18 Yea, and slew mighty kings: * for His mercy endureth for ever:
19 Sihon, king of the Amorites: * for His mercy endureth for ever;
20 And Og, the king of Bashan: * for His mercy endureth for ever;
21 And gave away their land for an heritage: * for His mercy endureth for ever;
22 Even for an heritage unto Israel His servant: * for His mercy endureth for ever.
23 Who remembered us when we were in trouble: * for His mercy endureth for ever;
24 And hath delivered us from our enemies: * for His mercy endureth for ever.
25 Who giveth food to all flesh: * for His mercy endureth for ever.
26 O give thanks unto the God of heaven: * for His mercy endureth for ever.
27 O give thanks unto the Lord of lords: * for His mercy endureth for ever.

1 By the waters of Babylon we sat down and wept, * when we remembered thee, O Zion.
2 As for our harps, we hanged them up * upon the trees that are therein.
3 For they that led us away captive, required of us then a song, and melody in our heaviness: * "Sing us one of the songs of Zion."
4 How shall we sing the Lord's song * in a strange land?
5 If I forget thee, O Jerusalem, * let my right hand forget her cunning.
6 If I do not remember thee, let my tongue cleave to the roof of my mouth; * yea, if I prefer not Jerusalem above my chief joy.
7 Remember the children of Edom, O Lord, in the day of Jerusalem; * how they said, "Down with it, down with it, even to the ground."
8 O daughter of Babylon, wasted with misery; * yea, happy shall he be that rewardeth thee as thou hast served us.
9 Blessed shall he be that taketh thy children, * and throweth them against the stones.

1 I will give thanks unto Thee, O Lord, with my whole heart; * even before the gods will I sing praise unto Thee.
2 I will worship toward Thy holy temple, and praise Thy Name, because of Thy loving-kindness and truth; * for Thou hast magnified Thy Name, and Thy word, above all things.
3 When I called upon Thee, Thou heardest me; * and endued my soul with much strength.
4 All the kings of the earth shall praise Thee, O Lord; * for they have heard the words of Thy mouth.
5 Yea, they shall sing of the ways of the Lord, * that great is the glory of the Lord.
6 For though the Lord be high, yet hath He respect unto the

lowly; * as for the proud, He beholdeth them afar off.
7 Though I walk in the midst of trouble, yet shalt Thou
refresh me; * Thou shalt stretch forth Thy hand upon the
furiousness of mine enemies, and Thy right hand shall save
me.
8 The Lord shall make good His loving-kindness toward me;
* yea, Thy mercy, O Lord, endureth for ever; despise not
then the works of Thine own hands.

Twenty-ninth Day

Morning Prayer

Domine, probasti   Psalm 139

1 O Lord, Thou hast searched me out, and known me. *
Thou knowest my down-sitting, and mine uprising; Thou
understandest my thoughts long before.
2 Thou art about my path, and about my bed; * and art
acquainted with all my ways.
3 For lo, there is not a word in my tongue, * but Thou, O
Lord, knowest it altogether.
4 Thou hast beset me behind and before, * and laid Thine
hand upon me.
5 Such knowledge is too wonderful and excellent for me; * I
cannot attain unto it.
6 Whither shall I go then from Thy Spirit? * or whither shall I
go then from Thy presence?
7 If I climb up into heaven, Thou art there; * if I go down to
hell, Thou art there also.
8 If I take the wings of the morning, * and remain in the
uttermost parts of the sea;
9 Even there also shall Thy hand lead me, * and Thy right
hand shall hold me.
10 If I say, "Peradventure the darkness shall cover me"; *
then shall my night be turned to day.
11 Yea, the darkness is no darkness with Thee, but the

night is as clear as the day; * the darkness and light to Thee are both alike.

12 For my reins are Thine; * Thou hast covered me in my mother's womb.

13 I will give thanks unto Thee, for I am fearfully and wonderfully made: * marvelous are Thy works, and that my soul knoweth right well.

14 My bones are not hid from Thee, * though I be made secretly, and fashioned beneath in the earth.

15 Thine eyes did see my substance, yet being imperfect; * and in Thy book were all my members written;

16 Which day by day were fashioned, * when as yet there was none of them.

17 How dear are Thy counsels unto me, O God; * O how great is the sum of them!

18 If I tell them, they are more in number than the sand: * when I wake up, I am present with Thee.

19 Wilt Thou not slay the wicked, O God? * Depart from me, ye blood-thirsty men.

20 For they speak unrighteously against Thee; * and Thine enemies take Thy Name in vain.

21 Do not I hate them, O Lord, that hate Thee? * and am not I grieved with those that rise up against Thee?

22 Yea, I hate them right sore; * even as though they were mine enemies.

23 Try me, O God, and seek the ground of my heart; * prove me, and examine my thoughts.

24 Look well if there be any way of wickedness in me; * and lead me in the way everlasting.

Eripe me, Domine   Psalm 140

1 Deliver me, O Lord, from the evil man; * and preserve me from the wicked man;

2 Who imagine mischief in their hearts, * and stir up strife all the day long.

3 They have sharpened their tongues like a serpent; *

adder's poison is under their lips.
4 Keep me, O Lord, from the hands of the ungodly; *
preserve me from the wicked men, who are purposed to
overthrow my goings.
5 The proud have laid a snare for me, and spread a net
abroad with cords; * yea, and set traps in my way.
6 I said unto the Lord, "Thou art my God, * hear the voice of
my prayers, O Lord.
7 O Lord God, Thou strength of my health; * Thou hast
covered my head in the day of battle.
8 Let not the ungodly have his desire, O Lord; * let not his
mischievous imagination prosper, lest they be too proud.
9 Let the mischief of their own lips fall upon the head of
them * that compass me about.
10 Let hot burning coals fall upon them; * let them be cast
into the fire, and into the pit, that they never rise up again."
11 A man full of words shall not prosper upon the earth: *
evil shall hunt the wicked person to overthrow him.
12 Sure I am that the Lord will avenge the poor, * and
maintain the cause of the helpless.
13 The righteous also shall give thanks unto Thy Name; *
and the just shall continue in Thy sight.

Evening Prayer

Domine, clamavi   Psalm 141

1 Lord, I call upon Thee; haste Thee unto me, * and
consider my voice, when I cry unto Thee.
2 Let my prayer be set forth in Thy sight as the incense; *
and let the lifting up of my hands be an evening sacrifice.
3 Set a watch, O Lord, before my mouth, * and keep the
door of my lips.
4 O let not mine heart be inclined to any evil thing; * let me
not be occupied in ungodly works with the men that work
wickedness, neither let me eat of such things as please
them.

5 Let the righteous rather smite me friendly, and reprove me; * yea, let not my head refuse their precious balms.
6 As for the ungodly, * I will pray yet against their wickedness.
7 Let their judges be overthrown in stony places, * that they may hear my words; for they are sweet.
8 Our bones lie scattered before the pit, * like as when one breaketh and heweth wood upon the earth.
9 But mine eyes look unto Thee, O Lord God; * in Thee is my trust; O cast not out my soul.
10 Keep me from the snare that they have laid for me, * and from the traps of the wicked doers.
11 Let the ungodly fall into their own nets together, * and let me ever escape them.

Voce mea ad Dominum   Psalm 142

1 I cried unto the Lord with my voice; * yea, even unto the Lord did I make my supplication.
2 I poured out my complaints before Him, * and showed Him of my trouble.
3 When my spirit was in heaviness, Thou knewest my path; * in the way wherein I walked, have they privily laid a snare for me.
4 I looked also upon my right hand, * and saw there was no man that would know me.
5 I had no place to flee unto, * and no man cared for my soul.
6 I cried unto Thee, O Lord, and said, * "Thou art my hope, and my portion in the land of the living.
7 Consider my complaint; * for I am brought very low.
8 O deliver me from my persecutors; * for they are too strong for me.
9 Bring my soul out of prison, that I may give thanks unto Thy Name; * which thing if Thou wilt grant me, then shall the righteous resort unto my company."

1 Hear my prayer, O Lord, and consider my desire; *
hearken unto me for Thy truth and righteousness' sake.
2 And enter not into judgment with Thy servant; * for in Thy
sight shall no man living be justified.
3 For the enemy hath persecuted my soul; he hath smitten
my life down to the ground; * he hath laid me in the
darkness, as the men that have been long dead.
4 Therefore is my spirit vexed within me, * and my heart
within me is desolate.
5 Yet do I remember the time past; I muse upon all Thy
works; * yea, I exercise myself in the works of Thy hands.
6 I stretch forth my hands unto Thee; * my soul gaspeth
unto Thee as a thirsty land.
7 Hear me, O Lord, and that soon; for my spirit waxeth faint:
* hide not Thy face from me, lest I be like unto them that go
down into the pit.
8 O let me hear Thy loving-kindness betimes in the
morning; for in Thee is my trust: * show Thou me the way
that I should walk in; for I lift up my soul unto Thee.
9 Deliver me, O Lord, from mine enemies; * for I flee unto
Thee to hide me.
10 Teach me to do the thing that pleaseth Thee; for Thou
art my God: * let Thy loving Spirit lead me forth into the land
of righteousness.
11 Quicken me, O Lord, for Thy Name's sake; * and for Thy
righteousness' sake bring my soul out of trouble.
12 And of Thy goodness slay mine enemies, * and destroy
all them that vex my soul; for I am Thy servant.

Thirtieth Day

Morning Prayer

Benedictus Dominus   Psalm 144

1 Blessed be the Lord my strength, * Who teacheth my hands to war, and my fingers to fight:
2 My hope and my fortress, my castle and deliverer, my defender in Whom I trust; * Who subdueth my people that is under me.
3 Lord, what is man, that Thou hast such respect unto him? * or the son of man, that Thou so regardest him?
4 Man is like a thing of naught; * his time passeth away like a shadow.
5 Bow Thy heavens, O Lord, and come down; * touch the mountains, and they shall smoke.
6 Cast forth Thy lightning, and tear them; * shoot out Thine arrows, and consume them.
7 Send down Thine hand from above; * deliver me, and take me out of the great waters, from the hand of strangers;
8 Whose mouth talketh of vanity, * and their right hand is a right hand of wickedness.
9 I will sing a new song unto Thee, O God; * and sing praises unto Thee upon a ten-stringed lute.
10 Thou hast given victory unto kings, * and hast delivered David Thy servant from the peril of the sword.
11 Save me, and deliver me from the hand of strangers, * whose mouth talketh of vanity, and their right hand is a right hand of iniquity:
12 That our sons may grow up as the young plants, * and that our daughters may be as the polished corners of the temple;
13 That our garners may be full and plenteous with all manner of store; * that our sheep may bring forth thousands, and ten thousands in our fields;
14 That our oxen may be strong to labor; that there be no

199

decay, * no leading into captivity, and no complaining in our streets.
15 Happy are the people that are in such a case; * yea, blessed are the people who have the Lord for their God.

Exaltabo te, Deus   Psalm 145

1 I will magnify Thee, O God, my King; * and I will praise Thy Name for ever and ever.
2 Every day will I give thanks unto Thee; * and praise Thy Name for ever and ever.
3 Great is the Lord, and marvelous worthy to be praised; * there is no end of His greatness.
4 One generation shall praise Thy works unto another, * and declare Thy power.
5 As for me, I will be talking of Thy worship, * Thy glory, Thy praise, and wondrous works;
6 So that men shall speak of the might of Thy marvelous acts; * and I will also tell of Thy greatness.
7 The memorial of Thine abundant kindness shall be showed; * and men shall sing of Thy righteousness.
8 The Lord is gracious and merciful; * long-suffering, and of great goodness.
9 The Lord is loving unto every man; * and His mercy is over all His works.
10 All Thy works praise Thee, O Lord; * and Thy saints give thanks unto Thee.
11 They show the glory of Thy kingdom, * and talk of Thy power;
12 That Thy power, Thy glory, and mightiness of Thy kingdom, * might be known unto men.
13 Thy kingdom is an everlasting kingdom, * and Thy dominion endureth throughout all ages.
14 The Lord upholdeth all such as fall, * and lifteth up all those that are down.
15 The eyes of all wait upon Thee, O Lord; * and Thou givest them their meat in due season.

16 Thou openest Thine hand, * and fillest all things living with plenteousness.

17 The Lord is righteous in all His ways, * and holy in all His works.

18 The Lord is nigh unto all them that call upon Him; * yea, all such as call upon Him faithfully.

19 He will fulfill the desire of them that fear Him; * He also will hear their cry, and will help them.

20 The Lord preserveth all them that love Him; * but scattereth abroad all the ungodly.

21 My mouth shall speak the praise of the Lord; * and let all flesh give thanks unto His holy Name for ever and ever.

Lauda, anima mea   Psalm 146

1 Praise the Lord, O my soul: while I live, will I praise the Lord; * yea, as long as I have any being, I will sing praises unto my God.

2 O put not your trust in princes, nor in any child of man; * for there is no help in them.

3 For when the breath of man goeth forth, he shall turn again to his earth, * and then all his thoughts perish.

4 Blessed is he that hath the God of Jacob for his help, * and whose hope is in the Lord his God:

5 Who made heaven and earth, the sea, and all that therein is; * Who keepeth His promise for ever;

6 Who helpeth them to right that suffer wrong; * Who feedeth the hungry.

7 The Lord looseth men out of prison; * the Lord giveth sight to the blind.

8 The Lord helpeth them that are fallen; * the Lord careth for the righteous.

9 The Lord careth for the strangers; He defendeth the fatherless and widow: * as for the way of the ungodly, He turneth it upside down.

10 The Lord thy God, O Zion, shall be King for evermore, * and throughout all generations.

Evening Prayer

Laudate Dominum   Psalm 147

1 Praise the Lord, for it is a good thing to sing praises unto our God; * yea, a joyful and pleasant thing it is to be thankful.
2 The Lord doth build up Jerusalem, * and gather together the outcasts of Israel.
3 He healeth those that are broken in heart, * and giveth medicine to heal their sickness.
4 He telleth the number of the stars, * and calleth them all by their names.
5 Great is our Lord, and great is His power; * yea, and His wisdom is infinite.
6 The Lord setteth up the meek, * and bringeth the ungodly down to the ground.
7 O sing unto the Lord with thanksgiving; * sing praises upon the harp unto our God:
8 Who covereth the heaven with clouds, and prepareth rain for the earth; * and maketh the grass to grow upon the mountains, and herb for the use of men;
9 Who giveth fodder unto the cattle, * and feedeth the young ravens that call upon Him.
10 He hath no pleasure in the strength of an horse; * neither delighteth He in any man's legs.
11 But the Lord's delight is in them that fear Him, * and put their trust in His mercy.
12 Praise the Lord, O Jerusalem; * praise thy God, O Zion.
13 For He hath made fast the bars of thy gates, * and hath blessed thy children within thee.
14 He maketh peace in thy borders, * and filleth thee with the flour of wheat.
15 He sendeth forth His commandment upon earth, * and His word runneth very swiftly.
16 He giveth snow like wool, * and scattereth the hoarfrost

like ashes.
17 He casteth forth His ice like morsels: * who is able to abide His frost?
18 He sendeth out His word, and melteth them: * He bloweth with His wind, and the waters flow.
19 He showeth His word unto Jacob, * His statutes and ordinances unto Israel.
20 He hath not dealt so with any nation; * neither have the heathen knowledge of His laws.

Laudate Dominum   Psalm 148

1 O praise the Lord from the heavens: * praise Him in the heights.
2 Praise Him, all ye angels of His: * praise Him, all His host.
3 Praise Him, sun and moon: * praise Him, all ye stars and light.
4 Praise Him, all ye heavens, * and ye waters that are above the heavens.
5 Let them praise the Name of the Lord: * for He spake the word, and they were made; He commanded, and they were created.
6 He hath made them fast for ever and ever: * He hath given them a law which shall not be broken.
7 Praise the Lord from the earth, * ye dragons and all deeps;
8 Fire and hail, snow and vapors, * wind and storm, fulfilling His word;
9 Mountains and all hills; * fruitful trees and all cedars;
10 Beasts and all cattle; * creeping things and flying fowls;
11 Kings of the earth, and all peoples; * princes, and all judges of the world;
12 Young men and maidens, old men and children, praise the Name of the Lord: * for His Name only is excellent, and His praise above heaven and earth.
13 He shall exalt the horn of His people: all His saints shall praise Him; * even the children of Israel, even the people that serveth Him.

1 O sing unto the Lord a new song; * let the congregation of saints praise Him.
2 Let Israel rejoice in Him that made Him, * and let the children of Zion be joyful in their King.
3 Let them praise His Name in the dance: * let them sing praises unto Him with tabret and harp.
4 For the Lord hath pleasure in His people, * and helpeth the meek-hearted.
5 Let the saints be joyful with glory; * let them rejoice in their beds.
6 Let the praises of God be in their mouth; * and a two-edged sword in their hands;
7 To be avenged of the nations, * and to rebuke the peoples;
8 To bind their kings in chains, * and their nobles with links of iron;
9 To execute judgment upon them; as it is written, * "Such honor have all His saints."

Laudate Dominum   Psalm 150

1 O praise God in His sanctuary: * praise Him in the firmament of His power.
2 Praise Him in His noble acts: * praise Him according to His excellent greatness.
3 Praise Him in the sound of the trumpet: * praise Him upon the lute and harp.
4 Praise Him in the timbrels and dances: * praise Him upon the strings and pipe.
5 Praise Him upon the well-tuned cymbals: * praise Him upon the loud cymbals.
6 Let every thing that hath breath * praise the Lord.

The End of the Psalter